GREENWICH VILLAGE STORIES

Greenwich
Village
Society for
Historic
Preservation

Universe

Edited by
Judith
Stonehill

GREENWICH VILLAGE STORIES

Greenwich Village Door. Photo by Alexandra Stonehill. 2013.

FOREWORD

Nearly a century ago, on a winter night in 1916, John Sloan, Marcel Duchamp, and four fellow artists climbed to the top of the Washington Square Arch and declared that Greenwich Village was now a Free and Independent Republic. More of a caper than a revolution, this became a Village legend—one of many—celebrating the bold ideas and stubborn individuality found here.

Walking through the Village is to brush against immortality. Henry James is still a presence in Washington Square, as is W. H. Auden on St. Marks Place. History is vivid and alive on these streets, where Eugene O'Neill and James Baldwin, Dawn Powell and Bob Dylan, Willa Cather and Jack Kerouac, Djuna Barnes and Jean-Michel Basquiat once lived and worked.

Our cherished neighborhood is no longer as creative and raffish these days, or so it's said, but there are many things that seem unchanged in the Village. Its remarkable architecture is protected, thanks in great part to GVSHP, and every corner of the area is filled with small cafes and restaurants,

small businesses that have been family-owned for generations, multitudinous small gardens, very small jazz clubs, and all those small streets with names instead of numbers—including Jane and Cornelia, Minetta and Stuyvesant. The place still casts a spell, as is evident in *Greenwich Village Stories*.

This collection of stories was written by contemporary Village artists, musicians, writers, photographers, performers, directors, designers, architects, historians, restaurateurs, and other neighborhood habitués, who each describes a memory, or impression, that shows the special character of Greenwich Village. Their storytelling is exuberant, poignant, lyrical, eclectic, and captivating, just like the Village itself.

—Judith Stonehill

Village finial. Photo by Alexandra Stonehill. 2013.

INTRODUCTION

The Greenwich Village Society for Historic Preservation was founded in 1980 to protect the architectural and cultural heritage of Greenwich Village, the East Village, and NoHo. We fight for landmark and zoning protections for our neighborhood to help preserve its history and character, and we oppose inappropriate and out-of-scale new development. We work to protect the independently owned businesses, and the small theaters, arts spaces, and performance venues that help define our communities. We document the works of cultural and preservation pioneers who inspire us, from Jane Jacobs to Merce Cunningham. And we provide research and resources to scholars and schoolchildren, residents and merchants, property owners and government officials, to inform them about the Village's unique history, its built environment, and its cultural legacy.

This is no small task, especially when one considers the vastness of that heritage, how much change it has undergone, and how much pressure it faces every day.

Landmark designations and zoning protections, though challenging to secure, can at least ensure the perpetuation of that special physical fabric. But culture, while inevitably intertwined with that physical fabric, is more ephemeral, harder to quantify, and even more difficult to preserve.

But never underestimate the power of the written word, or the resonance of personal stories. The cultural dynamism found in the Village has touched countless people across the globe. What follows are the voices of a few of those it has reached, and a few of its sources of inspiration.

—**Andrew Berman**
Executive Director
Greenwich Village Society
for Historic Preservation

CONTRIBUTORS

West 10th Street, with Jefferson Market Library. Painting by Frederick Brosen. 2012.

JONATHAN ADLER

If I lived above 14th Street I'd be a regional

sales manager for an office supplies concern. But I'm one of the lucky ones, one of the Chosen. The magical fairy dust of the Village settled on my shoulders and I became a potter.

It's 1993. I get fired. Again. Of course I deserve it. I'm a terrible employee. Personal calls, chronic tardiness, serial affairs with coworkers . . . and bosses! Do I despair? No! I'm a Village person. Nobody in the Village has a job; everyone has a calling. The Village is an alternative universe where any creative dream can become a reality. The Village is Oz. I tromp on over to Greenwich House on Jones Street, sign up for a pottery class, and begin my odyssey.

At the Greenwich House Pottery School. Photo by Alexandra Stonehill. 2013.

Café Wha? on MacDougal Street. Photo by Robert Otter. 1963.

PENNY ARCADE

When I was twelve years old in New Britain,

Connecticut, I went to the Palace Theater every Sunday afternoon to see the double feature. The movie I remember best because it was my favorite was called *A Bucket of Blood*. It was about an unsuccessful painter in a place in New York City called Greenwich Village who becomes a famous sculptor when he discovers a dead cat and covers it in clay. He liked being successful so much that he starts killing people and covering them with clay, too. When he wasn't killing people he went to a café full of poets and artists, beatniks in black berets and turtleneck sweaters. I felt drawn to the crooked streets and alleyways where the movie took place and I watched the movie over and over.

I asked my mother if she had ever been to Greenwich Village, because I knew she used to go to New York a lot when she was young and unmarried. She answered in her thick Italian accent that Greenwich Village was full of Italians and was where my father's two brothers, Uncle John and Uncle Nick, lived. I was elated because now there was proof that I had a real connection to this special place. I said, "Really? That's exciting," and my ma said, "What's exciting? It's a slum." When I was sixteen, fresh from reform school in the spring of 1967, Tony Norris who lived a few streets away called and said, "Some of us are driving to New York to go to the Village. Do you want to come?" I said, "Yes" and we drove for a long time and when we got there it was dark. We went to a place called Cafe Wha? A big bear of a man named Dave Van Ronk played guitar by himself and sang Joni Mitchell's song "Both Sides Now," a song she had written but had yet to record. Then the Paul Butterfield Blues Band took the stage and I can barely describe the excitement of hearing a live blues band for the first time and knowing I was in Greenwich Village. I looked around the cellar club but there were no beatniks there, or at least no one was wearing a beret.

Six months later I came back to New York with another sixteen-year-old kid named Mark McCarthy. I told the taxi driver, "Take us to Greenwich Village" and he dropped us on the corner of Bleecker and Thompson. I called the only person

I knew in the city, Johnny Pepin, and he said, "Oh no, you have got it all wrong. Come to East 7th Street and Avenue B." Today, the landmarked sign of the Village Gate across from the very spot on Thompson and Bleecker, where the taxi first dropped me, has my name on it. It reads: Penny Arcade: Politics, Sex & Reality. Destiny, I suppose. I never left New York after that. From that very first night I went to live in what was starting to be called the East Village even though everyone knew that it was really the Lower East Side. When I was young, the Village, both East and West, was a different place, of small, dark, barely lit bookstores and cafés where people went religiously each night to talk politics, read poems, play chess and music. New York was then made up of very clear-cut neighborhoods, not homogenized in any way, either socially or politically. Downtown New York stood in stark contrast to uptown in its bohemian values and more European way of life.

Yet in important ways, metaphysical ways, perhaps, it is not really so very different now, in its essence or in the people who are drawn here. For years now, when I don't know what to do with myself, I walk from East 8th and Avenue B across to the Hudson River, sometimes walking the side streets, sometimes just staying on 8th until it becomes Christopher Street, or I wander the back streets of the East Village and Lower East Side. There are many paths through my spiritual and emotional landscape, and I walk them wordlessly, communing with those like-minded souls of history who walked where I walk now, and I too intend to walk here after I am gone. This is a source of pure joy to me, and a comfort, and gives the Village its vibe.

Luc Sante wrote in his wonderful history, *Low Life*: "New York, which is founded on forward motion and is thus loathe to acknowledge its dead, merely causes them to walk, endlessly unsatisfied and unburied, to invade the precincts of supposed progress, to lay chill hands on the heedless present, which does not know how to identify the forces that tug at its rationality." The Village is populated by amazing spirits. Energy cannot be lost, and the energy of the unique and eccentric beings of the past resonates in our streets, and people visiting and living here today can experience it, too. If you walk to MacDougal Street and turn onto Minetta Lane, you will find Minetta Street, a half-moon alley. And until recently, if you walked to the middle of the street and looked up at the restaurant across the way, you could see faded letters reading Fat Black Pussy Cat. This famous beatnik haven, on a crooked street, could have been the café of my favorite film. Graham Greene said, "There is always one moment in childhood when the door opens and lets the future in.

Portrait and Poem Painting. Painting by Larry Rivers in collaboration with Frank O'Hara. 1961.

MARIO BATALI

I opened Pó at 31 Cornelia Street on

May 27, 1993, and my first and fondest memories emanate from that most excellent corner of Cornelia and Bleecker. On Sundays, intoxicated by both the bells of Our Lady of Pompeii and the fragrance of Zito's Bakery, I would wander out the front door of Pó at 9 a.m., having done all the prep for lunch and dinner, and head over to Faicco's to buy fixings for our Sunday staff supper. I'd chitchat with the boys behind the counter, sometimes trade recipes with the sweet Village ladies on the way to or from confession, but mostly guarantee a delicious meal for the crew and me after night service. One of my faves was a sugo with braciole, sausages and spareribs that I would cook slowly on the back burner and serve around 11 p.m. with gnocchi or rigatoni. After Faicco's I'd pick up some nice ripe taleggio at Murray's Cheese directly across the street. Right next door I'd grab a couple of still hot loaves of Zito's poetic, sesame-coated "Italian bread" and then maybe peek into the Aphrodisia herb store to smile at my favorite cats. If I still had time, I'd grab a box of *sfogliatelle* for the crew for breakfast and snag an espresso with a little anisette at Rocco's, just because it was Sunday. A constitutional around Father Demo Square, a look into the kids' park at Winston Churchill Square to make sure there were no sleepers bothering the kids, and a morning salutation to Joe at Joe's Pizza, still the best slice in the Village if you get the fresh mozzarella for a seventy-five-cent upgrade. Up Bleecker past the steps of the church and back into my kitchen for a great day making lunch or dinner for my local family and theirs.

Ruggiero's Fish Market (detail), on Bleecker Street.
Photo by Robert Otter. 1965.

Brabeium.

e

a

d

c

b

c

J.E.Deseve Del.

Benard Direxit.

HISTOIRE NATURELLE, *Botanique.*

LAUREN BELFER

Decades ago, when I moved to New York

after graduating from college, I stayed in a one-room apartment at the corner of Barrow and Bedford that my aunt and uncle rented for their plants. Their passion for horticulture had overwhelmed their small home across the street, and rather than leave their beloved neighborhood in search of a larger apartment, they'd opted to divide the collection. In return for free rent, I cared for *Aglaonema commutatum*, *Chlorophytum comosum*, and *Cissus rhombifolia*, among many others, as well as a fruit and vegetable garden on the fire escape.

That summer, I worked as a low-paid, temporary filing clerk at an art gallery uptown. Just out of college, with no career prospects, I was, in a bleak and terrifying sense, lost. During lunch hours, I interviewed unsuccessfully for whatever openings the employment agencies found for me. I filled the long evenings by walking through the Village, trying to find my way. In those summer days of gay liberation, exquisitely muscled men in tight t-shirts and jeans loitered along Christopher Street. The presence of these men, none of them interested in me, made me feel safe. The acrid odor of incinerator soot filled the air. WQXR incessantly advertised the new musical *A Chorus Line* with its plaintive refrain, "Who am I, anyway? Am I my résumé?" The questions stung every time I heard them.

On a Friday evening in August, after a particularly dispiriting week of interviews, I returned home alone, facing a weekend without plans. Soon I'd be unemployed. I pushed open the wooden gate on Barrow Street and entered an arched passageway lined with garbage cans. The passageway opened onto a courtyard, and the renowned former speakeasy at the far side of the courtyard gave off sounds of merriment. But I opened a door just inside the passageway. Although I locked this door each time I departed and arrived, I always found it unlatched. Before me rose a

Botanical Print. Circa eighteenth century.

stairway so narrow that I had to turn sideways to fit. The soft, indented steps tilted first to the right, then to the left, then to the right, as if I were walking on a listing ship. The walls were sticky. I grasped the railing. One flight, two, three, four, and down the hallway, with its peeling paint, to the plant apartment.

The floor of the plant apartment listed, too, toward the three long windows with their open view. My aunt had chosen the apartment because of its good sunlight, and she didn't permit an air conditioner. As the summer wore on, the top-floor studio had become oppressively hot and humid, and the plants had grown to jungle-like proportions. To reach my bureau, I made my way around thriving specimens of *Ficus elastica* and *Ficus lyrata*, *Nephrolepis exaltata*, *Crassula ovata*, and *Dracaena marginata*, the labels prepared in my aunt's concise printing. After changing out of my work clothes, I clambered out the window onto the fire escape to collect the day's harvest for my aunt and uncle. Cherry tomatoes, scallions, lettuce, zucchini. Because of the soot, the harvest had to be soaked in Ivory liquid and thoroughly rinsed before eating. So said my aunt. I wasn't tempted to take samples.

A band of orange struck the fire escape's ironwork. I looked up. The raking light of sunset was brilliant upon the rooftops of the townhouses and tenements all around me. The light glinted upon the windows of the pre-war apartment buildings, igniting the glass like fire. As the wind picked up, a breeze cooled my bare arms. Suddenly I was breathing the scent of the sea. And at that moment, I felt no need to worry about what the future would bring me. I was home.

AVIS BERMAN

My version of Greenwich Village vanished

before I was born. It was constructed in my imagination, materially aided by some real bricks, stucco, and mortar. As a young writer, I was searching for the history of the Whitney Museum of American Art when it was a small gallery with a big heart, and located in four conjoined townhouses on West 8th Street. I found that history in the testimony of artists, in photographs and memoirs and, most palpably, in the building that now houses the New York Studio School of Drawing, Painting & Sculpture, at 8 West 8th Street.

In the Studio School's galleries and work spaces, the past remained alive precisely because it maintained such an active present—the place was crowded with students and it smelled of paint, turpentine, coffee, and clay. Walking through the school, I reveled in recognizing elements of the building's past as the Whitney's original site. Here was the gallery where John Sloan had his first solo show, here was the way to Charles Sheeler's old rooms. One passage led to Gertrude Vanderbilt Whitney's living area and another to the studio where Daniel Chester French created his model for the Lincoln Memorial. Even scraps and fragments of the former museum evoked so much beyond themselves. A trompe l'oeil door concealed the entrance to a staircase linking the museum's offices and Whitney's private quarters, protecting the museum's founder from importuning calls upon her person—and her purse. Several walls were stenciled in stylized eagles and stars and stripes—the eagle was the Whitney Museum's insignia in the 1930s, an emblem of its unswerving championship of American art.

On the fourth floor was a battered bit of gray pigment, the only leftover of an infamous mural commission. Juliana Force, the Whitney's first director, had a lavish duplex apartment that stretched across the third and fourth floors of the museum. Decorated with Aubusson rugs, Victorian furniture, and modern paintings, it served as a grand stage for the legendary parties that took place after openings. In 1932, Force let Thomas Hart Benton, in lieu of money he owed her, create

eight mural paintings for her library. Benton chose to forget that the murals were produced in exchange for a loan. He accused Force and the Whitney of cheating him, and a controversy arose. Just before the Whitney moved away from 8th Street in 1953, the murals were sold and it was difficult to extract them cleanly. That remaining corner of one of Benton's panels reminded me of the clash they engendered, yet it made me marvel more at the larger story involved. Art torn from its roots might never be restored, but the history of the Whitney itself, though similarly parted from its Village home, was still traceable within those walls.

At the New York Studio School. Photo by
Daniel Gerdes. 2008.

JENNIFER FINNEY BOYLAN

East Village, fall of 1980. Reagan had just

been elected, and I decided, the hell with everything, I'm moving to New York. I arrived at Port Authority with a backpack containing one spare t-shirt and Neal Cassady's book, *The First Third*. In the other hand, I had an Autoharp. I figured that there wasn't anything they could throw at me that I couldn't counter with either the Cassady or the Autoharp. My friend Peter met me at the station, and we took the subway—my first—to Astor Place. We walked to a bar called the Grassroots Tavern, which was on St. Marks Place. I think it's still there. He sat me down at a table and we drank a pitcher of beer. Peter gave me a big map of Manhattan, which we unfolded on the table, and he marked it up with a felt-tip pen, explaining what each neighborhood was, where it was safe for me to walk, where it wasn't. Over some places he drew a skull and crossbones, which meant Don't Ever Walk Here, Ever. Then he gave me one subway token, which I think cost fifty cents. The city was mine.

The next day we got lunch at a diner called the Waverly, a block from Washington Square. The waitress turned out to be this girl I'd had a relationship with in high school. She invited me back to her house that night, a place way uptown, where I slept on the floor. The next morning, we learned the apartment next door to hers was empty—the occupants had just moved out. A quick bribe of the super and I was living there. I needed a roommate, though—so my old friend asked a guy she knew if he wanted to live with me. He turned out to be a young filmmaker named Charlie Kaufman. Charlie and I became roommates, and we spent our days typing on our typewriters. He got a job working as a production assistant on a Woody Allen movie, which turned out to be *Zelig*. Years later he made *Adaptation* and *Being John Malkovich* and *Eternal Sunshine of the Spotless Mind* and all those mind-bending movies.

I sat in that apartment playing the Autoharp. It was a good thing I'd brought it. I didn't really know what life was going to be for me, but I knew that it would involve a lot of singing.

Astor Place. Photo by Rudy Burckhardt. 1948.

TOM BURCKHARDT

I grew up on East 14th Street and Third

Avenue in the 1970s and it was kind of hairy. Of course, as a kid, you have no real idea: it seemed normal, and only afterwards do you find different contexts and see that not everybody lived like that.

There were certain innate skills I had then, such as judging if the junkies on the nod would fall in a slow motion or stagger to the right so I could navigate past them, and learning how to push our front door open when a passed-out drunk was blocking it. We lived over the Jefferson Theater and I remember knowing that I couldn't walk on 13th Street, that it was dangerous territory.

Then, twenty years later I moved there. In 1995, my wife Kathy and I moved to a storied artist's loft building that stretches from 13th to 14th Street. I suddenly had all this room to work in, so I now had the ability to make something larger. You wanted the ambition of your work to measure up to that magnificent space.

I've become the unofficial historian of 404 East 14th Street and have uncovered stories of wild parties, biblical floods coming down from the roof, lawsuits, and, most of all, stories of the legendary art that was created here. Its history as a creative place dates from the 1960s when Larry Rivers, Claes Oldenburg, Yayoi Kusama, On Kawara, and John Chamberlain first colonized the building. Richard Hell, Jean Dupuy, and Allen Ginsberg all lived here at various times. Fred Wilson and Whitfield Lovell have been my upstairs neighbors for years.

I'm ambivalent about the changes in the East Village. On one hand I have raised kids here who haven't been mugged, like I was, but it's also gotten a bit too straight for me. Artists certainly can't afford to live in our building now. It's hedge fund guys who are moving in, so it seems a lot less creative. New York has always marched on, good and bad, and it's worth remembering not to get all cranky about this. There's still a lot of gritty charm in our neighborhood.

Postmen. East Village. Photo by Saul Leiter. 1952.

Charles Street Portals. Painting by Andrew Jones. 2005.

GRAYDON CARTER

In an age of cities,
there is just one village
that is known by people the world over:

Greenwich Village.

It got there by being small.
Let's keep it that way.

MARTHA CLARKE

The first time I came to the Village was in the

spring of 1957. My dance teacher from Baltimore brought me to see *The Threepenny Opera* at the Theater de Lys on Christopher Street. It turned out to be an auspicious occasion.

It has been both a blessing and a curse to choose the stage as a livelihood. Actually it has been more like a love affair: lots of drama.

My work has been presented at several wonderful theaters in the Village: New York Theatre Workshop, the Public, and Minetta Lane. Like the Village, these theaters have an intimacy and atmosphere that is special to this part of the city. They have been here a long time, like well-loved antiques, still very serviceable and full of personality and history.

In 1965 I married and moved to a delightful floor-through apartment on West 13th Street. I studied ballet at the nearby Joffrey School on West 10th—then came a year in Rome. When my son, David, was born, we moved to the country in northwestern Connecticut. I came back to the Village after my divorce. For the past twenty-five years I have had an airy and elegant apartment on West 10th Street, the former home of Marcel Duchamp. My bed resides on the spot where Duchamp kept his chess table.

The Village has a unique character. I love its scale and intimacy: the old houses and gardens, the atmosphere of fashionable and funky shops and restaurants, the presence of the NYU campus. The Village has a wonderful raw energy that mixes with its history. I love the expanse of sky that can be seen from nearly anywhere.

Greenwich Village has been a constant in my life ever since I saw *The Threepenny Opera*. I now look forward to directing my own production of this Brecht/Weill masterpiece not far from the Theater de Lys where it all started for me more than fifty years ago. Full circle.

Washington Mews. Photo by Alexandra Stonehill. 2013.

PATRICIA CLARKSON

I have a million Beaux stories, but the one

I'd like to share happened at the very end of his life. I have lived in Greenwich Village for twenty-three years. And for roughly fifteen of those years, I walked my beloved dog, Beaux, through the streets of the Village. We traveled every inch of this great neighborhood. I often joked that he could give a walking tour. He really did know where Eleanor Roosevelt lived. And of course, we got to know many neighbors, two-legged and four-legged.

Sadly, toward the end of his life, he lost most of the use of his back legs. So I'd wrap an old pashmina around the back end of his body to support his hind legs, and hold it as he walked. This glorious dog who had once traversed this neighborhood became confined to a third of a block. In a beautiful way, though, I found that people started to come to him.

One day, after I'd just finished walking him, I put him safely in my apartment and went back down to run errands. At the door of my co-op building, I found a handsome young man in gym clothes with a greeting card in his hand.

"I was just about to slip this card for you under the door of your building," he said. "I work out at the gym across the street. I watched you carry your dog up the block and back. I was so moved by your plight that I got off my treadmill and went around the corner to buy you a card."

I was overwhelmed and thanked him profusely. I thought to myself, who would do such a thing? Surely, he must be an actor who knows who I am, or he recognizes me, or maybe he's a fan. As he walked away, I glanced down at what he had written on the envelope. It simply said, *for the lady with the dog*.

Washington Square Serenade. Drawing/collage by
Tony Fitzpatrick. 2008.

KAREN COOPER

In January 1992, I moved with my husband,

George Griffin, and our nine-year-old daughter, Nora, from East 4th Street to West 4th Street.

East 4th and the Bowery had become ragged and raucous, an uneasy meeting of the remaining alcoholic/homeless population, the spate of new bars and audio stores, and the growing numbers of NYU students. Moving to West 4th, even on the *wrong side of the tracks* (west of Eighth Avenue), brought us in contact with streets whose storied names still have a timeless appeal: Jane and Christopher, Bank and Bethune, Perry and Charles.

My favorite neighborhood route: along the famously ungrid-like West 4th Street from Eighth Avenue to Seventh. As you walk past the mysterious neon palm tree that has been in a ground-floor window all these years, the memory of Lanciani—that great patisserie and neighborhood fixture for so long—returns. There's the nowhere-to-be-seen canoe-shaped window box on the facade of the long-gone travel agency that once anchored a corner near the Stinky Sock, a shabby, hardworking laundromat. But much remains as it was. Looking toward the river, down those narrow streets, I see rows of townhouses, silent, elegant, and dignified veterans of more than a century. In the spring, sitting outside at one of Tartine's handful of tables, there is always the sound of birds roosting in the ivy on the building across the street. A block away—at a restaurant whose name changes every few years—I recall watching the snow come down as George and I took a break from unpacking so many years ago. I felt I had moved to an idyllic, never-never land. I still do.

West 4th Street. Photo by Alexandra Stonehill. 2013.

SIMON
DOONAN

In 1985 I scored a job working for Diana

Vreeland at the Costume Institute. I was hired as "display designer" on a show titled *Costumes of Royal India.*

I was living in L.A. at the time. Lacking the funds to rent an apartment in New York, I slept on the floor—of the hallway—of a friend's apartment on Second Avenue and 11th Street. This gentleman was named John Badum.

John was the quintessential Village eccentric. He was, in many ways, the downtown freaky version of Vreeland. He knew everyone from Dianne Brill to Marc Jacobs to Leigh Bowery to David LaChappelle to Iggy Pop and was more than happy to drop names and to introduce all and sundry.

In appearance John was a cross between Mama Cass and Orson Welles. He was fat and fabulous and regal, and enormously proud of the glossy mane of jet-black nipple-length hair that followed him down the street.

John worked in the Garment District selling a successful line of washed-silk sportswear called Go Silk. He was highly esteemed in the fashion world, but his real vocation was fulfilled in the evening hours. He'd founded a club for himself and his camp followers called the Disco Modeling School. Outings took place on a weekly basis and involved matching satin outfits, lots of booze, vintage platform shoes, and the occasional run-in with law enforcement.

One night I came home from a grueling day of szhooshing saris to find that John had invited forty people over and that we were all going to wear fluffy Patsy Cline wigs and go hang out at Area. "It's performance art, girls! Now shut the fuck up and get your wigs on."

When John entertained he would fill the bath with ice and sprinkle blue food dye all over it. He would then jam a dozen bottles of champagne into the melting

East Village Wall Art. Photo by Alexandra Stonehill. 2013.

blue iceberg and invite everybody in his phone book. He was Auntie Mame. He was a punk-rock Elsa Maxwell. He was Holly Golightly + Liberace + Courtney Love.

A self-invented super-funster, John epitomized everything that was great about the Village in the pre-hedge-fund era. Affectionate and welcoming, wildly unpredictable, kind and wicked, naughty and irreverent, he was an aristocrat of reckless fabulosity who made you think anything was possible. In other words, he *was* Greenwich Village.

When my Vreeland gig ended, John introduced me to Gene Pressman, the owner of Barneys: "You cannot go back to L.A. You need to get your shit together and go work for Barneys." (Twenty-seven years later I'm still there.)

John's apartment was always bursting with tarty girls and naughty boys, artists and models, and moochers and boy-toys. He had a soft spot for good-looking blokes. His reckless, open-hearted generosity eventually caught up with him. In 1999 he was murdered by one of his lovers.

Whenever I walk past his old building I always look up to pay homage and remember the fun and the madness of that period. In my mind's eye I can see John and his glossy black hair sitting in the window, smoking a doobie, and trying to attract the attention of passing New Yorkers with a squeaky-toy crocodile he kept on the sill for that very purpose.

LINDA ELLERBEE

The very first day I moved to Greenwich

Village (July 1978), a tourist stopped me on the street and asked me for directions to Washington Square. I thought to myself: I must look like a person who lives in Greenwich Village.

I was, I admit, thrilled that this was so.

Being from Texas, most of what I knew about the Village came from books, plays, and movies. Some of it was even right. But it was a romantic view, mine. It still is. I like my romantic picture of the Village, even if I now know it not to be accurate. If it ever was.

But as there is no constant but change, it's not surprising that my Greenwich Village refuses to stay fixed in any orbit. This is both pleasing to me, and sad, and sometimes confusing. I'm not conflicted about having Ralph Lauren on Bleecker Street (I hate it), but do I miss the druggies who populated the park near my house? I do not.

I miss the really cheap but good restaurants, the street musicians, the Lion's Head, Shopsin's (and Kenny Shopsin), the *old* Minetta Tavern, the head shops, the Pioneer grocery store (replaced first by Banana Republic, which sold no bananas, and then by American Apparel, which also sold no bananas), the . . . well, I could go on, but so could we all.

I live in a nineteenth-century house on a tree-lined brownstone block across the street from a park with a baseball diamond, handball court, playground, and pool. There is also an indoor pool, basketball court, track, and a branch of the public library. But none of these things is new, shiny, enclosed by glass, or costs a lot to use. They are public. I like the sound of that word. *Public.* This is important because, although sometimes it seems as if it is, the Village is *not* a gated community.

It remains, in spite of everything, a neighborhood. We know or at least recognize each other, many of us. Sometimes we fight. Sometimes we party. Often we take care of one another.

Once upon a time, I got myself into money trouble (my soon-to-be-ex-husband took most of mine), and although I was a well-paid network correspondent on national television, I was in danger of not being able to make the next mortgage payment. A neighbor, a woman much older than I, who lived in a tiny apartment and worked as a legal secretary, said not to worry, she would lend me the money, and she did. It was her entire savings. Think about that. I do. She's dead now, but to me she'll always be a big part of what makes the Village the Village: *a big, loud, beating heart.*

I raised my two kids in that house, and I still live there. Not only did I pay back my neighbor within three months, I paid off my mortgage within thirty years. I would not want to live anywhere else in the city. When people from other neighborhoods are out of town and are asked where they live, they say, "New York."

I say, "I live in Greenwich Village."

West 9th Street. Photo by Alexandra Stonehill. 2013.

Portrait of Allen Ginsberg on his East 7th Street apartment roof. Photo
by William Burroughs. 1953.

LARRY FAGIN

1959?

In the middle of one of those nights John Stevens and I
drove all the way from D.C. to the Village
just to get a hot dog
I guess D.C. was out of hot dogs
we must've been desperate
& I wound up crashing
on Tim Craig's floor
ground floor Cornelia(?) off W. 4th
Hugh Romney was (talking)
at the Gaslight
I met LeRoi and Hettie Jones
in déclassé Chelsea
tried out the drinks at Minetta Tavern
heard William Morris (not *the* William Morris
or the Agency) read a poem at the Gaslight
"in the silver blue of the mothering sea" (phooey)
but Allen Ginsberg handed me some important papers
to do *what* with?
too stoned to remember
John Brent at the Gaslight
or Van Ronk
& now I forget where on MacDougal
the Gaslight is (was)
were you there then?

I couldn't get enough money together
for Sonny Rollins at the Vanguard
which still pisses me off
people were so *cheap*
but I sampled opium for the first time
huddling in some eastside Ukrainian doorway
stoned standing up!
(I think!)
we never did get those hot dogs
anyway Stevens freaked me out & I ran away
to Philadelphia with his wife
somewhere in that time frame
but came back to stay with Ray Jenkins
on Avenue D!
now was *that* avant-garde or what?
we ate subsistence-style
fried baloney sandwiches

KAREN FINLEY

For Historic Preservation:

Walking through the Arch
In Washington Square Park
A nod to nonconformity
Before the yellow curve and a billion sold
With a bird's-eye view of once a hanging
And 20,000 buried remains

The land given to freed slaves
Though there was a catch
Your children will be born as slaves
The cruelty and horror proclaimed
Amidst the benches and forced green
Stolen landscape from the Lenape

Oh hello historic preservation
A fountain, players of chess
As we welcome the
Bulldoze of the university for 2031
In the spirit of Robert Moses
Demolition for progress eminent

The lone Louis Sullivan building
At 65 Bleecker Street
With the ornamentation of terra-cotta
Always take a moment

Yet cringe at the renovation of retail
In aluminum modern rape

The facade never suffices
When the heart of the building is
Removed
Ah that word renovation
A lobotomy
More like it

Right now as I write this
At Performance Space 122
At 9th and First Avenue
Renovated, gutted
An autopsy *performed*
Organs dissected as bitter porcelain

Corinthian columns interfered with sight lines
Memento Mori seating discarded curbside
Mahogany built in drilled and scrapped
Luminous ecru ceiling lamps departed
The beveled windowpane whistled off-key
Keep the interior poetic alive we weep

Floors of wood, classrooms with slate and tile
A stained glass held for safe keeping reads;
"Every waking hour we weave
whether we will or no
every trivial act or deed
into the warp must go"

But I am certain in some future date
With laments and hindsight

Such as with the former Penn Station

Ah, historic preservation —What would Jackie do?

As we whisper in the 4 corners at Grand Central

100 years old today

Alphabet City. Photo by Dona Ann McAdams. 1987.

TOM
FONTANA

The Circle Repertory Company was an

outstanding incubator for many of America's best emerging playwrights. For a long time, the group was located in an old garage on Seventh Avenue.

As a novice writer, I eagerly attended each production. But one night, the scene on the street was more compelling than the evening's performance.

Lillian Hellman was there, in all her cigarette-smoking, cinder block, imperial radical glory. She, of *The Little Foxes* and *The Children's Hour*. She who would not cut her conscience to fit the year's fashions. I had just read *Pentimento* and I was in awe, afraid to approach her, yet wanting somehow to be acknowledged by the same eyes that had beheld Dashiell Hammett and Dorothy Parker. I thought of clever things to say, I thought of lighting her next cigarette, I thought of jostling her septuagenarian body. In the end, I did nothing but stare.

For me, Lillian Hellman represented all that is wonderful, difficult, brilliant, irritating, and impossible about living in the Village. She was a talented writer, yes; political troublemaker, yes; but more important, she was a survivor. And though she is long dead, Lillian Hellman still walks the streets of Greenwich Village, as do so many of the talented, tortured, complex artists who have lived, labored, and played here.

Snow. East Village. Photo by Saul Leiter. 1960.

AMANDA FOREMAN

The first time I saw Greenwich Village

I was thirty years old and madly in love. Newly married and looking for our first home together, my husband and I found a fourth-floor walk-up on 12th Street. The stairs almost killed us, but on reaching the top we were rewarded with a double-height loft space with wooden beams, exposed brick walls, and a working fireplace. We felt as though we had stumbled onto a film set representing what a Village apartment is supposed to look like. It was a living fantasy. Inside the apartment all was light and serenity. Outside was the noisy modernity of Manhattan.

Six months after moving in we celebrated the New Year's Eve of the Millennium. Two geese, ten pounds of potatoes, a bushel of corn, a basket of broccoli, and a baker's dozen of baguettes were hauled up the stairs in preparation for the great feast. When dinner was ready, fourteen of us sat down at a table illuminated only by candlelight. The evening wore on in a golden haze of bonhomie until suddenly someone noticed that it was two minutes to twelve. We rushed up the escape ladder to the rooftop, expecting to hear the roars of a city seething with energy. We stood still and heard . . . nothing. The magic of 12th Street was to be in the moment and yet in another time all of our own making. We sang songs and hugged one another on the roof, sending our voices up into the night sky.

West 11th Street Railing. Painting by Andrew Jones. 2005.

City at Twilight, from Fifth Avenue and 12th Street. Painting by Jane Freilicher. 2010.

JANE FREILICHER

Everyone who was anyone in the art

world during the late 1940s seemed to study with Hans Hofmann. His school was right above a movie house on 8th Street near Sixth Avenue. It was one floor up and that's where the classes took place every morning. We drew from a model most of the time. Students from all over the country came to study there, including a hard-core group of young painters like myself. Hofmann was charismatic and funny. He was the guru. He had tics from his German background—*Nicht* this and *Nicht* that. The young artists who studied there included Nell Blaine, Larry Rivers, Michael Goldberg, Wolf Kahn, Robert De Niro Sr., Paul Resika, among many others.

I first lived in a modest apartment way over in the East Village on 11th Street, where I painted views from my windows. After I married Joe Hazan, we bought 16 West 11th Street—a house just off Fifth Avenue, built in 1845—from the Sullivan family, who had owned the house since 1883. When our daughter Lizzie was born, we moved to an apartment nearby, but kept the house and rented it out. On March 6, 1970, the house next door to ours—18 West 11th—exploded. Young radicals from the Weathermen had been making bombs in the basement. Although we weren't living there at the time, we heard the noise of the explosion blocks away. It was a disaster. We stood behind the police barricades in disbelief. There is a newspaper picture of Joe and our tenant Dustin Hoffman moving furniture out of the building. The city condemned the property and wanted us to tear it down, but we had an architect file papers and fought to preserve it. We succeeded and rebuilt the house. Whatever needed to be done was done. We restored the exterior and saved the interior.

I feel comfortable in the Village. I have lived in my apartment on Fifth Avenue and 12th Street since 1965. It has a great studio—an old greenhouse—with views more or less in every direction. I have painted these views for years, never tiring of them.

BETTY FUSSELL

May 1949. Grand Central Terminal was
confusing enough with buffalo herds stampeding me down the black hole of
a subway entrance and onto a train where I clung for dear life to a strap. Wow.
Riverside, California was never like this.

I was groggy anyway from six days and five nights in a window seat on the
Santa Fe El Capitan from Los Angeles to Chicago and then the 20th Century Limited
via the Hudson River to New York. Wow. What a country. What a river. What a sky-
line the dawn lit just before we plunged underground.

When I emerged, eventually, from a maze of black holes, stairs, tunnels, and
incomprehensible signs, the first thing I saw was a maze of streets. But the signs on
the odd triangular building right in front of me read loud and clear—Village Cigars.
I smiled and went in for a pack of Camels.

Where I came from, the Devil ruled Hell through tobacco and alcohol, but
here, wherever I looked, everyone was carrying a lit cigarette. And there were all
these little bars with people lined up drinking in the daytime! Wow. I was going to
like this place.

And that's how I discovered the Village, my Village—through a cigar store.
When I moved back to California sixty years later, after living half that time in the
converted Greek Revival Presbyterian Church on 13th Street between Sixth and
Seventh Avenues, I meant to buy a final cigar to pay my respects. But Hurricane
Sandy interfered and I was lucky to fly out between storms. Hail and farewell to
Village Cigars, still on Seventh Avenue, a true survivor.

MARGARET HALSEY GARDINER

I made it to the Major Leagues. Well, not really. But for a thirteen-year-old girl, it felt like it.

I grew up in the MacDougal-Sullivan Gardens in the 1950s and '60s—the days of bohemians and Beats and artists and poets and free thinkers.

From nursery school through eighth grade, I attended Grace Church School, on Fourth Avenue and 10th Street. Grace was coed and had a boys' baseball team coached by Myron Jones—Mr. Jones to me—who also taught English. We adored him. He was the rare teacher who could make *A Tale of Two Cities* compelling to sixth-graders.

Back to baseball. In the spring of 1962, for eighth-grade sports we played baseball in the afternoon out in the schoolyard. I played first base. Seems I was pretty good, because when it came time for the team's first game of the season, against Allen-Stevenson, a private boys' school uptown, Mr. Jones took me aside and said he wanted me to play on the team. They needed me on first base—couldn't win without me. You can only imagine how it made me feel. I was a *girl* and Mr. Jones was asking *me* to play on the *boys'* team? It was ten years before Title IX and a year before *The Feminine Mystique*. These were the days of Betty Draper, not Friedan.

But here's the best part. He told me I was really good and it just wasn't fair that I couldn't play on the team, so we'd fool them. All I had to do was wear pants and put my hair in a ponytail and hide it in a baseball cap.

Only in the Village, I say. (Thank you, Mr. Jones.)

MALCOLM GLADWELL

I came to New York City to be the New York

correspondent for the *Washington Post* in 1993. I think I had been to New York once before. I knew almost nothing about the city, except what I had gleaned from Martin Scorsese movies. Someone I knew gave me the name of a broker in the West Village named Ted, and one February afternoon I took the train up from D.C. to look for an apartment.

I called Ted at 10 a.m. He seemed slightly out of breath. "Where are you?" he asked, immediately. "Are you far away?" I said I wasn't. "Something has just come in," he said, with what I would recognize only much, much later—to my deepest regret—as urgency. "It will be gone by noon."

The apartment was, as I recall, on Barrow or Morton. We were the first in the door. I looked around. I liked it. The views! But, as I explained to Ted, I didn't know New York at all. I hadn't seen any other apartments. What was so special about this "West Village"? How could I make a decision based on a single data point? (I was coming from Washington, D.C.; that is how we spoke.)

I passed. Ted looked at me like I was on crack. In case you are wondering, it was a charming, top-floor, rent-regulated, $1,100 a month, two-bedroom with a south-facing terrace.

Christopher Park with statue of General Philip Sheridan.
Photo by Alexandra Stonehill. 2013.

MIMI GROSS

My father, Chaim Gross, had a studio at

63 East 9th Street in Greenwich Village for more than thirty years, from the time
before I was born until I became a young teenager. Earlier, he had also lived in a loft
over the studio. John Graham, the painter and collector of African art, lived next
door. Willem de Kooning worked across the street.

Every morning my father would ride his bicycle downtown from South
Harlem, where our family lived, to his Village studio, in an old brownstone building
with a front stoop. One went up the steps and through a long dark hallway into a
large square studio space, with high ceilings and a skylight, a wall of windows in the
back, and a small yard behind. The worktable was under the windows, tools were
hanging up all around, and logs of wood were piled in corners.

Figurative sculptures in both wood and marble, of every size, were rhythmi-
cally placed so that the eye always had an object that it could see. The sculptures
were placed on all kinds of wooden market boxes and an assortment of pedestals.
A short distance away from the windows, the room became very musty, dark, and
mysterious. In one corner there was a big brown desk with piles of papers and
books, a small light, and a radio permanently tuned to the Yiddish station, WEVD.
In the middle of the room there was a potbellied stove that in the winter was always
burning, making the room warm and cozy. Along the walls hung a variety of
framed watercolors and drawings by Chaim's friends. Under the skylight, and close
by the stove, was a work stand where my father would carve: chip, chip, chip, chip.
The sound of my childhood memory.

For many years, every Saturday afternoon, friends and fellow artists, writers,
and photographers would gather at his studio, an informal salon. My father would
continue carving (he called it "chiseling") while everyone else hung around talking,

Chaim Gross in his Studio. Photo by Alfredo Valente. 1938.

flirting, drinking. I was like a studio brat, trying to make conversation about things I knew nothing about. Sometimes I would take out my crayons and draw.

Some of the characters I remember were the photographers, the group from *Life* magazine, in particular Eliot Elisofon and Arnold Newman. The artist Moses Soyer—who lived just a block away—and his twin brother, Raphael, would often come by. Other artists, all good friends, were Federico Castellón, Milton Avery, Robert Gwathmey, Abraham Walkowitz, Philip Evergood, John Graham, Fletcher Martin, David Burliuk. The art collectors Hudson Walker and Joseph Hirshhorn talked about what was new at the auction houses and at the exhibitions. Harold Rome and Irwin Hersey, who each collected African art, came by to eagerly share their recent finds. And then there were the Yiddish writers. My uncle Naftoli Gross, a poet writing for the daily newspaper, *The Forward*, seemed to know everyone from the Yiddish literary world—including both of the Singer brothers, Sholem Aleichem's son, and many others whose names I have forgotten. There were women, too: my mother and her best friend and cousin Roz Roose, students of my father, or girlfriends of the various visitors. As a kid, I particularly remember that everyone was always smoking!

My memories of the Village are various, layered over many years. Yet the fresh scent of the new wood chips is still so vivid and evocative, I can easily imagine myself back in my father's studio.

JOHN GUARE

In 1953, for my fifteenth birthday, my parents

took me to the Leonard Bernstein, Comden and Green musical *Wonderful Town*. By the time the opening number—"Here we live, here we love, right in the heart of Greenwich Village"—was over, I knew my heart's destination.

It took eleven years for me finally to arrive home.

I got out of the Air Force Reserves in 1964, came back to New York hoping to live a life writing plays. But where to start? Even Off-Broadway was an unspeakably distant planet. I went to the Village to roam around and ended up at the Bleecker Street Cinema to catch up on the latest French flick that I had missed while defending my country the past six months.

I found myself on a funny diagonal street called Cornelia Street right off 4th Street that I had never been on before. Three-quarters of the way down the block near Bleecker, I stopped. In a storefront window, a handmade poster announced a new play called *The Madness of Lady Bright* by somebody named Lanford Wilson. The storefront was a coffee house called the Caffe Cino.

I looked inside and saw a long dark narrow room filled with small round tables and wire-back chairs placed around a space in the center. It was decorated like an attic in hell with Christmas lights and big posters of Maria Callas and Jean Harlow on the walls and a mad jumble of paintings. It was like standing at the edge of the sea. I wanted to be there. People sat in the back. "I'm a playwright," I called into the dark. Someone said, "Cino is here at 6 p.m." I came back the next day at 6 p.m. carrying the few plays I had written. Joe Cino was a swarthy bulky Sicilian wearing a dashiki and doing something to a large espresso machine at the bar. I said "Hello? I'm a playwright." He said, without looking up, "I'm not doing any new plays unless they're by Aquarians." I gulped. "But I'm an Aquarian." He stopped tinkering. He looked at me suspiciously. "Prove it." I fumbled for my wallet and took out my driver's license. He took it. "Hmmm. February 5, 1938. I've been looking for you." He unrolled a chart on the counter and ran his fingers over dates and astrological symbols. "You open 10th of May, run for two weeks and look! You have a one-week extension!"

And that's how I made my New York debut as a playwright. I don't know what would have happened to me if I'd been born in October.

I found my first apartment a while later on the corner of West 10th Street and West 4th Street where those streets collide in a burst of Village logic. I lived in a four-story walk-up with a twenty-foot ceiling and skylight, wood-burning fireplace, eat-in kitchen, bathroom with a tub and shower, looking out into a bunch of backyard gardens. The rent? $32 a month. The previous tenants were two sisters who had lived there for forty years at $22 a month.

I found out Lanford Wilson lived cater-corner to me on the 4th Street side and knew him by this time. I'd open my window and sit there violently tapping the keys of my typewriter to torment him or he'd do the same to torment me.

In 1973, John Lennon and Yoko Ono moved out of their apartment at 105¼ Bank Street up to the Dakota and I got the apartment, which had been a sculptor's studio built in the garden. It had a thirty-foot ceiling with skylights and a spiral staircase up to the roof. That rent was a massive $500 a month. Pilgrims who didn't know their idol and his wife had moved uptown flocked to my door and left me love letters.

My life had a happier end. Two years later I met my wife who lived on 12th Street. I moved in with her. We still live there and hope to be carried out many years from now. I've had the same phone number for all these years; my answering machine still says you've reached CH 2 [for Chelsea]. I miss the Bleecker Street Cinema, the 8th Street movie theater, that Italian restaurant that had the bocce ball court in its center, the Bitter End, the Caffe Cino, Sutter's bakery, the Phoenix bookstore, Jefferson Market, and Jack Delaney's steakhouse in Sheridan Square. (I wonder if the neon horses still gallop under the Starbucks sign.) Today I love the fountain in Washington Square, love all of the park and walk my dogs there every night and sometimes run into Jessica Lange or Sam Shepard or Larry Kramer doing the same or F. Murray Abraham coming home from a show. We catch up on the latest lowdown and then I go home to Adele and look forward to waking up in the morning and going to my computer and working on a play. I'm on the ninth floor so nobody hears me type.

Bleecker Street Cinema. Photo by Robert Otter. 1965.

High Line train running on elevated tracks through what is now Westbeth. 1936.

ROBERT HAMMOND

I graduated from college in 1993, and the
next year I moved to the West Village, attracted to the industrial character of the
area. It had old and new residential buildings. It had the Hudson riverfront, which
had not yet been transformed into a park. The piers were still rotting.

There is a bar a few blocks from my old apartment called Automatic Slim's.
On the wall outside is a 1930s black-and-white photo of a freight train on an elevated track running through a factory building. Across the street is the building
itself, with a remnant of the track at the third-floor level. I used to stop and look at
the picture and then look up at the building. I liked the idea that a train used to run
through my neighborhood.

I spent some time in the Meatpacking District—I'd go to Florent—and I had
seen parts of the railway in that neighborhood. And I had gone to a few galleries in
Chelsea and seen it cross over the streets there. But I didn't know that all those bits
and pieces were connected and called the High Line.

The summer of 1999, I read a piece in the *Times* that said that Mayor Giuliani's
administration was trying to tear down the High Line. There was a map, and you
could see that the tracks were continuous, a mile and a half of rail running right
through Lower Manhattan. That's what really got me interested, the idea that this
industrial relic had lasted so long and was about to be dismantled. I decided to get
involved.

My first thought was that I could help someone who was already working to
save it. This is New York, and in New York everything that could ever be threatened
has a group associated with it, right? So I started making calls and discovered that a
local community board was sponsoring a public hearing in August.

I was off from work that week, out on Fire Island, and I actually came back
from the beach to go to that meeting. I had never been to a community board
meeting. I had never had any desire to go to a community board meeting.

There were maybe twenty people there, and we heard a presentation by the Regional Plan Association, which had been commissioned by CSX, the railroad that owned the High Line. They discussed different options, from demolition to using it for freight to making a park up on top of it.

After that, people got up and spoke about why it was a bad idea to repurpose the High Line. It was a blight on the neighborhood. It was going to fall down any day. It was holding up the economic development of the area. It was dangerous. It was dark underneath. A whole litany of arguments, and really vehement. I was surprised at how strongly these people felt. I had been thinking about speaking at the meeting, but not after all that.

I stayed behind afterward, trying to find anyone else interested in saving the High Line. There was no one except the guy who had been sitting next to me. He told me his name was Joshua David.

I said, "Well, you know, I'm very busy, but if you start something, I could help." And he said, "Well, I'm also very busy. Maybe you should start something." We exchanged business cards and agreed to talk later.

Jane Street Area (detail). Painting by Rudy Burckhardt. 1958.

Washington Square Arch. Photo by Robert Otter. 1962.

NAT HENTOFF

In 1953 I became the New York editor of
Down Beat—then the world's leading jazz magazine. I lived in Greenwich Village and
found so much swinging there. I soon learned, for instance, when tourists asked
where to find the best jazz clubs, to tell them not to miss the Village Vanguard,
where they'd never be disappointed.

At a small club nearby, a large, round, unknown alto saxophonist asked to sit
in one night and brought joy to me and all the other listeners. In a couple of weeks
"Cannonball" Adderley had a record contract and the start of his international
career. And on another night, I'll never forget John Coltrane at the Village Gate surprising himself and us for two hours, deepening the same composition with such
passionate invention that it felt like a religious experience, and I'm an atheist.

Along with my *Down Beat* gig, I suddenly had a jazz fan's dream fulfilled. I
was asked to direct and produce sessions for a new record label, Candid Records.
Writing about jazz is always a kick, but sending the music out into the world was so
gratifying, especially after I heard what Max Roach, Abbey Lincoln, and Coleman
Hawkins were doing at the Village Gate as the civil rights movement was cresting
around the nation.

In Max Roach's *Freedom Now Suite*, the raw roots of our Jim Crow history and
the rising, driving liberation rhythms breaking it down made me ask Max if any
established record label had asked to record it. To my surprise, none had, and we all
went into the studio. Soon after its release in 1960, as an album called *We Insist!*, we
were pleased to learn that it was banned in South Africa.

Both on and off the stand, there is much to learn from these players. As Charlie
Parker used to say: "Music is your own experience, your thoughts, your wisdom. If
you don't live it, it won't come out of your horn."

Once, as Thelonious Monk and I were talking, a young saxophonist-composer
I'd known in Boston, Gigi Gryce, came by. Excitedly, he shouted to Monk, "I just got
into Juilliard!" In response, Monk defined jazz without saying the word: "I hope,"

he said to Gigi, "you don't lose it there."

Dizzy Gillespie, who became a close friend both during his Village gigs and elsewhere, taught me about my work when he told me what he discovered about his own: "It's taken me much of my life to know what notes *not* to play." At the start of what would become fifty years at the *Village Voice*, writing about education and civil liberties, I'd gone on and on until I joined Dizzy in that self-discovery.

I am still in the Village and love living here more than other place in this city, because I can see the sky. But NYU is insistently circumscribing that.

This atheist also came to know a possible future Catholic saint in the Village, Dorothy Day. She staged a Vietnam draft protest in 1965 very near here, in Union Square. And I was there. There are still a lot of constitutionally self-governing citizens in the Village.

DAVE HILL

The Village—will we ever really understand it?

I ask this not in a figurative, rhetorical, or even existential sense, just in a way that attempts to address how the corner of West 4th Street and Eighth Avenue manages to sit north of the corner of West 12th Street and Eighth Avenue without fail every single time I leave my building. And while I pride myself on having a fairly reasonable understanding of how the streets of my neighborhood map out, I take even greater pride in watching strangers ask the very next person they see for directions immediately after I've finished giving them my version. And ideally after that person tells them, they'll turn around and shoot me a dirty look regardless of how close to being right I might have been. Most of the time, I'll wait for it.

I moved to the Village in 2006, and—challenging topography aside—I'd be lying if I said I didn't enjoy pretty much every moment of it. Sure, there are those who will complain that the grit and vitality of the neighborhood was gone long before I talked my friend Mike into lugging all my worldly possessions up to my fifth-floor walk-up studio apartment. And that its streets are now home to little more than an endless string of muffin shops. But you know what? I like muffins. A lot. And if I keep my eyes peeled, I can still share one most early mornings with a statuesque beauty who goes by the name of Shoshanna but is known to area law enforcement as Curtis.

Adding to all of the above magic is the fact that Bob Dylan actually took the time to write a song about the street I live on. And the odds of that ever happening had I stayed in my native Cleveland really weren't very good at all. And who cares if that song appears to be about some major a-hole Bob once knew? I can barely understand a word that guy is saying anyway.

TONY HISS

In back of my Village apartment is an almost block-long garden laid out a hundred years ago by knocking together a series of private backyards. It's altogether remarkable, on an early spring morning, to look out of a third-floor bedroom window in the heart of Manhattan and see, at eye level, dozens of gold-and-black bumblebees bouncing among crimson and creamy-white apple blossoms while a couple of sharp-voiced blue jays chase each other over rooftop chimney pots.

The stars above shine as brightly during the day as they do at night—it's just that they're hidden from view during daylight hours by the brilliance of the sun. In Greenwich Village, once a separate hamlet north of New York, starlight—in the sense of continuity and steadiness and things that persist—is often easier to see than elsewhere in the city. It happens any foggy night, when the lights atop the Empire State Building disappear, or right after a big snowfall when silence is the only sound and the rest of the city recedes. Some famous and long-beloved New York blocks have very little star glow left. For instance, stand right next to the Empire State Building, and there are no hints that this was once the site of two opulent hotels, the Waldorf and the Astoria, which a little more than a century ago were the social center of New York.

I like to think that in the Village my block has its own starry distinction, one visible even on the brightest days. The garden is part of what more than two hundred years ago was the Randall farm, land that Captain Robert Richard Randall in 1801 bequeathed to a benevolent association he had set up, Sailors' Snug Harbor. The idea was that developing the farm would generate money to benefit elderly, indigent sailors. The rest of the farm, which stretches from Washington Square to 10th Street east of Fifth Avenue, has mansions and loft buildings and high-rise apartment houses. Nobody planned it that way, but the garden out back is probably the last piece of the original farmland that is still open space. The dirt, unexcavated, was never built on. So for at least the last seven generations, the view right here has only been of growing things. The seasons and the living landscape remain the touchstone.

Courtyard at ½ Fifth Avenue, with statue of Miguel de Cervantes.
Photo by Alexandra Stonehill. 2013.

BOB HOLMAN

Village

I live in the Village
Not just any Village
Not just every Village
Where the City
Becomes a Village
That's my Village
Where the intercontinental
Becomes the neighborly experiential
That's my Village
Uptown Downtown Lowdown Notown
That's the place that's Home Sweet Home Town
The Village is where I live

Jane Jacobs is my patron saint
She lived it with her apron paint
She made the stuff that's too obvious to see
The definition of reality
A mix, a mess, a mishegoss
Some trees in cement, some mental floss
To let ideas drip like a faucet
Honey trees growing in a bedroom closet

So as you walk down these concrete paths
Making your tantric plans to evanescence the globe
All ways Centered on this place's Energy Rocket

Why, that's simply the pulse of living here
All the lands and all the peoples and all the dream boats
Behind the blinking windows of these stacked buildings
The population froths in imagination syncopation
Utopic and grand, elegantly funked and plastered
It's a Village you are living in, all the way down
Hometown Lowdown—Mighty Squat Humanness
The Village is where I live

Izzy Young in NYC (detail), at his Folklore Center on MacDougal Street. Photo by David Gahr/Getty Images. 1960.

JAC HOLZMAN

In 1951 I found myself back in New York

from St. John's College, it having been suggested that my fondness for electronics instead of the Great Books was draining time from my classics studies.

My pre-Village life had been lived on the Upper East Side, but the predictability and emotional isolation was sucking the young life out of me. And the smug contentment of my parents was so different from the world seen by their nineteen-year-old son.

Adventure, and my future, clearly lay within the Village. I was fascinated by the improbable people, the wafts of sensuality that pointed to a possible nirvana of "free love." The Village represented everything to which I was drawn and so I first moved to 40 Grove Street, a rickety rooming house where I shared the fifth floor with four others in equally shabby circumstances. Rent was $5.00 per week (yes, the decimal point is correct), and if I stood and strained my arms to the fingertips of each hand I could just touch both walls at once. I moved in with a bed, clothes, wooden planks and cinder blocks for bookshelves, and a tiny TV. Well, the screen was tiny, but the set weighed thirty pounds and required that I tape one end of its "rabbit ears" antenna to a body part to capture a reasonable image.

The Village locals honored my privacy. My need for solitude came from the fear of not knowing who I was, or how to be. The neighborly ambience, local acoustic music, and optimism of my new community gently guided me to my emotional center and a place to grow my passion, a record label initially devoted to folk music I called Elektra Records.

HETTIE JONES

Sacred Ground

on the fifth of December a rose
blooms on Sixth Street. That rose,
Anna says, always that one
every winter only that rose

in the dooryard of the synagogue
once the Lutheran church

                    sacred ground
                    says the man
                    who approaches us

                    come inside I'll
                    show you more

meanwhile these leafy stems—
two hard-fleshed amber hips—
this blood red budding—

the bitter cold
wind streaming

East Sixth Street Synagogue. Painting by
Frederick Brosen. 2010.

Pier 49 at Bank Street. Painting by Peter Ruta. 1991.

DONNA KARAN

My husband, the artist Stephan Weiss,

loved Greenwich Village. He found an amazing industrial building on the corner of Greenwich and Charles Street, which he gutted and then designed and built as his studio. He added a bright, open living space on the second floor, as well as an enormous roof garden. The studio had a rugged, masculine vibe to it, which made it his.

Stephan went there every day, drawing, sculpting, and painting in as large a scale as he wanted. Because the space was huge, he was able to park his other passion in life—his Ducatis—inside. He loved the neighborhood and being part of it. He walked everywhere, knew everything and everyone. I loved being in the Village, too, and we even talked about moving over the studio, but decided that Stephan needed a separate workspace from home. The studio was our calm in the chaos—a private escape. To me, the Village is art, bohemia, beatniks, and freedom. It's like a little European enclave within the city, with everything human-scaled and no skyscrapers in sight.

After Stephan's death in 2001, his studio became the Urban Zen Center, and so the Village has become my home, too. Urban Zen can be described as a community center where people come and connect in forums and seminars, or visit art exhibitions. A retrospective of Stephan's work was recently shown in the very studio in which the work was created, which seems so appropriate. One of his last works, the massive, ten-foot-high bronze sculpture *Apple*, is installed in Hudson River Park, a short walk from the studio. As a friend of ours said, "Every day you see people enjoying Stephan's big perspective, as they walk by, or maybe touch, his great homage to his beloved city." Being in the Village holds so many memories for me. It's where I bring my family and friends and surround myself with love, and, of course, Stephan's art.

JONATHAN NED KATZ

As a kid growing up in Greenwich Village,

I had trouble with math and reading, but got praise from my parents for my art. On a trip to the Museum of Modern Art with my father in 1948, when I was ten years old, I was charmed by the primitive paintings of the self-taught artist Henri Rousseau. I said to myself, "I can do that. I can't paint realistic, but I can paint primitive."

As a young teenager I showed a portfolio of my work and was accepted at the High School of Music and Art as an art major. In 1955, when I was seventeen, I painted a picture of a shy, downward-glancing nun in Greenwich Village. I didn't know it then, but that nun was the perfect visual image of my repressed gay self.

In the 1960s I used my ability at art to make a living as a textile designer, starting at a studio where the owner and many of the other male artists were gay. But publicly I was playing straight. On June 28, 1969, when the Stonewall riots took place a few blocks from my apartment, the walls of my closet muffled the sound of change coming from the world outside.

But I finally left sexual repression behind and joined the fledgling gay liberation movement. In June 1972 I took a deep breath and used my real name as the author of *Coming Out!*, a documentary play produced by New York City's Gay Activists Alliance. This play led to a contract for my first book on LGBT history, *Gay American History: Lesbians and Gay Men in the U.S.A.* Over the next three decades I published three other books on sexual history, and later returned to creating art. Now, in my mid-seventies, I'm painting sexual history. In the spirit of the Stonewall rioters, I'm still kicking.

Washington Square. Photo by Michael Magill. 1993.

ROBERT KAUFELT

My passion for cheese prompted me to

buy the old Village cheese shop—Murray's—when the owner decided to return home to Calabria in 1989. I also had a secret agenda, which I was reluctant to share at the time. As I came of age in the Sixties, at the height of sex, drugs, and rock and roll, it was always a dream of mine to inhabit the neighborhood where Dylan and others had tread, as if somehow their vibe might rub off on me. But the clubs were disappearing. Things change, and only Dylan himself (and the Rolling Stones) are forever.

A little background: my uncle Jay taught me to play the guitar when I was a boy. I never made much progress, and so at the age of twenty-five I put the old Gibson down and forgot about it. In my early years behind Murray's counter, I met all sorts of interesting people; back then, only that sort lived in the Village. One of my favorite customers was the great old folk singer Dave Van Ronk, the mayor of MacDougal Street, who knew a lot about food and how to cook it. I was reluctant to let him know I was a fan from way back, and that his scratchy-voiced version of "Cocaine" still played in my brain long after my recreational drug years were over.

One day I got up the nerve to tell him I was a fan, and thinking of taking up the guitar again. He told me he gave lessons around the corner at his place on Sheridan Square, if I'd like to give it a go, and so I began my weekly lessons. Dave was, of course, the best finger-picker in America. It seems, however, that I had not much talent for the guitar after all, beyond a rudimentary level, and my lessons became a private time to listen to stories from a great raconteur. After a while, it was clear I was wasting my money, and he told me so.

When I told Dave I was fooling around with songwriting, he encouraged me to pursue it. It became a favorite hobby of mine, and when Dave died several years back, I was sorry he never got to hear the two CDs I'd recorded—all original tunes—with me singing and playing and sounding OK because my friend Steve, who produced and recorded them, is a real musician. I'm working on another CD

Drugstore Crows, on MacDougal Street. Photo by Jack Manning/Getty Images. 1966.

now, and sometimes, when I pick up my guitar—not as often as I'd like—I think of Dave, and Dylan, and all those singers and pickers who influenced my youth, and I'm grateful that I discovered a new life, my current life, on Bleecker Street in the Village. Now that the neighborhood is landmarked, the vibe is bound to linger for a while longer.

John Coltrane Jazz Album. 1960.

LENNY KAYE

Music in the air. Past the Village Vanguard

where Coltrane holds court. Down Greenwich Avenue where Pietro Deiro Jr. has an accordion school, taking up the lineage from his father and uncle. Along West 8th where Dayton's has the newest records in the window: The Fugs, Group Image, Cat Mother, Lothar and the Hand People. Just up the block from where Electric Lady aligns its recorders.

Along MacDougal. Washington Square, folk singers gathering around the fountain to imagine a more rural time, when all this was farmland. Nearing West 3rd, the Velvet Underground at the Bizarre to the left, the Magicians and Spoonful and UFO and Bloos Magoos echoing right, from the Night Owl. True stereo. Past the Cafe Wha?, where Jimmy James strolls out after playing a set with his Blue Flames, and heads toward the Cafe Au Go Go.

Take the local. The Gaslight, fingersnapping guitar strum or bongo poetry, making way for Scrap Bar metal. The Kettle of Fish, the liquid pleasures of swimming and drinking. Izzy Young's Folklore Center, a one-room schoolhouse. The Speakeasy where Fast Folk gather.

Coffee and existentialism at the crossroads of Bleecker and MacDougal, Fred Neil in the bull's-eye, con-eccentric circles. Left at the corner. Nobody's, a bar where the satin-and-spangle of the English style intermingle. Kenny's Castaways, imported from uptown, offering an open-hearted mic. The fortress of the Village Gate, Thelonious and Nina and Tito shaking its walls. The Cafe Au Go Go, where Jimmy (aka Jimi) goes to jam with John Hammond Jr., and the Blues Project cut their classic live. The Other End, once Bitter, where I'm backing John Braden for six weeks in my own first summer. He has a song called "W. 4th St.": *The train stops / the people rush up the stairs.*

Time to go to work. Village Oldies. 45s line the walls, albums, posters. Bleecker Bob and Broadway Al. Pull a record from the shelf and let it replay.

BRAD KESSLER

There'd been a hurricane the day before,

and in the morning a pigeon flew into our open roof door in the old PS 122 building. I shared a studio there on the top floor at 150 First Avenue. It was a crisp October morning. The pigeon arrived hungry and disoriented, looking for a place to rest. You could tell she was someone's pet, a slender pink and cream bird—what pigeon fanciers call a Persian High Flyer—with a blue ID band around one leg. She'd likely lost her flock during the storm. I tried to find her owner from the numbers on her ID band—to no avail. She could have come from anywhere, as far as Philadelphia or Delaware. I fed her bread and pigeon peas.

The first few days she perched on the roof's parapet and surveyed First Avenue, the strange low canyons of the East Village, the high glass cliffs around NYU. In the distance, across a craggy vale of concrete and brick, the Twin Towers rose in dusty autumn sunlight.

By the third day she started flying laps above the roof of PS 122, scribing tight circles like a cyclist on a small training track. The next day her circles grew wider. She'd soar south to Houston, bank west, then turn north above Broadway, rise to a pinpoint high above Union Square—lost momentarily in cloud—then rocket down Avenue A, stoop sharply and glide back through the open roof door, braking at the last second with a whirr of wings. She was thrilling to watch.

Each day that late October her flights grew longer until she'd be lost, not for minutes, but hours at a time. She was homing back to her flock—wherever it was— and she'd return in the early dusk to the East Village right around rush hour, tired and hungry. Inside the studio, after a meal, she'd fold her wings and sleep.

One afternoon she didn't return. The sun went down over the West Side. The lights came up on the Williamsburg Bridge. It was a clear pale twilight. Headlights crowded First Avenue. I searched the skies over 9th Street and over the trees of Tompkins Square Park. I kept going out to the roof to look for her. Finally, at full dark, I shut the roof door for the night and knew she wasn't coming back.

It's been years now, but I still think of that pink and cream high flyer and how she chose the East Village for her sanctuary. How, out of the million other rooftops, she picked PS 122 as her refuge, just as every kind of artist (painters, performers, dancers) had found refuge there for years. What other neighborhood in the world—what other *building*—was as welcoming to accidentals and outcasts, to those who'd lost their flock or never had one, offering them a place to pause for a few days or years or decades and find their voice, their legs, their wings?

ED KOCH

I moved to Greenwich Village in 1956.

My first apartment was at 81 Bedford Street and subsequently, 72 Barrow Street and later, 14 Washington Place, from which I moved to Gracie Mansion, the mayor's residence. There were lots of things to like about the Village. One was my involvement with Citizens for [Adlai] Stevenson, the predecessor political club to the Village Independent Democrats (V.I.D.). He was running for president of the United States at the time against Dwight Eisenhower. Stevenson's speeches have never been equaled in style or substance. They were thrilling. I campaigned for him nightly in Sheridan Square, standing literally and occasionally on a soapbox.

While that was a very involving activity for me, there was one other even more fulfilling: eating dinner. At that time, there were three restaurants that I regularly went to because the food was truly delicious and very cheap. The oldest of the three was Louie's, a bar in Sheridan Square in a building that is no longer standing. Louie's veal parmigiana was $1.75, and beer was a dime a glass. Another restaurant was the Limelight on Seventh Avenue, which had prix-fixe dinners for $1.80, which I think ultimately increased to $2.50. With a delicious three-course dinner, plus coffee, you also got the opportunity to peruse photographs in a gallery provided by the owner of the restaurant.

Then there was the Lion's Head on Christopher Street in Sheridan Square, near the offices of the *Village Voice*, where the food was superb and even more varied than the others and just as cheap, but not prix fixe. The reporters and authors of books, plus the politicians, made it their dinner table away from home. It is no longer there.

Later, when I was mayor, about 1978, a fourth restaurant, the Buffalo Roadhouse, opened on Seventh Avenue. I really loved it, especially during the summer, because it had outdoor space. Its hamburgers and soups have never been equaled, at least for me. I believe the owner wanted to upscale and changed to French cuisine. It ultimately closed, and I didn't miss it.

Ed Koch in Democratic Party Office, on Sheridan Square. Photo by Fred W. McDarrah/Getty Images. 1963.

With the passage of time, these recollections have become even sweeter and the food even better. I now live at 2 Fifth Avenue, right off Washington Square Park. I don't expect to move again.

RALPH LEE

From the very first Village Halloween

Parade, in 1974, there were two components to the event: masked and costumed performers moving through the streets with giant puppets, and other costumed individuals occupying fire escapes and front stoops, playgrounds and church steps, engaged in theatrical routines as the paraders marched by.

I directed the parade for its first twelve years, joining the spectators incognito and walking along with the revelers, checking to see that no giant puppets were falling apart, performers were doing their stuff, samba bands raising the temperature with their big drums, cops with their Dracula fangs in place for a quick smile. What dress-up theme had the School of Visual Arts come up with this year? Famous paintings? Playing cards? Landmark buildings? There was always a group of gay guys with fabulous ideas: dressing as Imelda Marcos's shoes, slices of pizza, or takeout Chinese.

Nine old crones on stilts were created for the front of the parade, sweeping away road rage and car fumes, preparing the streets for pedestrian frolic and bursts of individual imagination. Many residents along the route allowed our staff to invade their homes, set up lights, and fill their balconies and windows with strange and unlikely creatures. Or we would string clotheslines across the streets, with ghostly laundry frantically dancing in the night.

During the early years, the parade mobilized at Westbeth, the artists' community in the Far West Village. The start of the parade was signaled either by a smoking winged creature flying across Westbeth's courtyard on a wire, or by my son Josh rappelling down a wall dressed as a giant bug with threatening pincers. From there we marched to Abingdon Square, down Bleecker Street, east on Charles over to West 4th Street, winding our way to Washington Square.

Bleecker Street. Drawing by Saul Steinberg. 1971.

When the parade route changed, bringing us east on West 10th Street over to Fifth Avenue, we gained access to several historic buildings. At Jefferson Market Library, we created a giant spider to wriggle down from the balcony at the top of the library's storybook tower and filled the windows with silhouettes of spooks and goblins made by schoolchildren. On West 10th Street, we populated the balconies of Renwick Row with grotesque gentry.

As the parade marched down Fifth Avenue, a large fat devil welcomed the throngs from the top of Washington Square Arch. Once the crowd was in the park, the devil appeared to slide down into the fountain on a wire. For the finale, a forty-foot skeleton, held aloft by poles, was hoisted up into the Arch, where he could caper and shimmy. The skeleton was inspired by an old Elizabethan round called "The Ghost of Tom"—"long white bones with the skin all gone"—which, for me, was the theme of the parade.

As I walked with the crowds, I was always a bit bewildered. How did all this happen? I might have lit a match, but all this? It evolved rapidly, like a bonfire. So many people fanned the flames, seized on the idea, and brought their own high spirits to the parade.

.

JOHN LEGUIZAMO

So in the '80s I started coming down to

the Village to seek performance freedom. Rumor had it there were places doing a lot of non-linear, non-comedy-club-type performance. It was free. No joke requirements, no story or material constraints. You could be yourself. It sounded like everything I was looking for. I, like so many others, came to the Village to find myself. I started out doing a twenty-minute piece of revisionist history as if the Bible had taken place in Spanish Harlem instead of the Middle East. I played all the characters and they all talked to each other: Jesus, Mary Magdalene, Joseph, etc. To my surprise, people didn't leave. They actually stayed through it all, and to my astonishment they even laughed. I had found my "thing" and on top of it, a crowd that allowed me to explore comedy and storytelling in a different way than you saw on TV.

The places were mostly in Alphabet City, all the way east to Avenue A, which was a no-man's-land at the time. The names were unusual and so were the acts. Dixon Place was a first-floor apartment that belonged to Ellie Kovan. She'd open her front door and charge admission and we, the acts, would perform in her living room. We waited in her kitchen to go on. The Knitting Factory had a lot of jazz but also some acts. It was by invitation only, and the better you got, the more often you got asked back. Then you worked your way from last to early on the list. Scouts from the more exclusive venues would troll around and check you out, and if you passed muster then you'd get invited to places like PS 122—you had "made it" in the performance art scene if you appeared there. The Nuyorican Poets Cafe was legendary and too cool for school; Miguel Piñero, Miguel Algarín, and all the Miguels there with their Spanglish and hipper-than-hip vernacular were a huge influence on me. It was home to a new form of poetry, the slam. There was ABC No Rio, the H.O.M.E. for Contemporary Theatre and Art, Gas Station, and Gusto House, the freest of them all. I saw Reno, Michael Mayer, Eric Bogosian, Penny Arcade, Judy Gold, Danny Hoch, Karen Finley, Bill Callahan, David Cale, and Tom Murrin (Alien

Comic). Everybody pushed the envelope in themes, styles, and methods. Nobody was attached to any pre-existing format. We were making our mark and trying to break out of the old molds of performing and content. It was so exciting to be surrounded by such a creative community and you felt supported. You could do no wrong. I have never felt so inspired. You need to feel safe to fail and you have to feel able to fail in order to think outside the box.

Mambo Mouth. Poster featuring John Leguizamo. 1991.

"BRUTALLY FUNNY!"

—HOLDEN, THE NEW YORK TIMES

mambo

mouth

Written and performed by **JOHN LEGUIZAMO**

directed by **PETER ASKIN**

CALL: (212) 477-2477
TICKETRON: (212) 246-0102

ISLAND VISUAL ARTS
MARK GROUBERT   ELLEN M. KRASS
present

mambo mouth

A Savage Comedy

Written and Performed by
JOHN LEGUIZAMO

Directed by
PETER ASKIN

| Scenic Designer | Lighting Designer | Sound Designer |
| PHILIPP JUNG | NATASHA KATZ | BRUCE ELLMAN |

| Musical Supervisor | Executive Producer | Production Stage Manager |
| JELLYBEAN BENITEZ | ELIZABETH HELLER | JOSEPH A. ONORATO |

| Associate Producers | General Management | General Press Representative |
| MICHAEL SCOTT BREGMAN DAVID KLINGMAN | MARSHALL B. PURDY ENTERPRISES | CROMARTY & COMPANY |

WINNER! 1991 OUTER CRITICS CIRCLE AWARD!

WINNER! 1991 OBIE AWARD!

ORPHEUM THEATRE   2ND AVENUE & 8TH STREET

Design: FRAVER for LeDonne, Wilner & Weiner, Inc.   Photo: DAVID HUGHES

ANITA LO

The space that houses my restaurant,

Annisa, at 13 Barrow Street just east of Seventh Avenue South, has a storied past. I knew nothing of it when I took over the space in 2000, except for the fact that it had been a contemporary American restaurant called by its address, and then a short-lived reincarnation called One Three. I gathered bits and pieces of it over the years. Bill Murray stopped by one night with a friend, and after a drink or two, while gazing up at the vaulted ceilings, recalled coming here in the 1970s when it had been a café.

I learned the whole story at 184¾ West 4th Street, a shop around the corner too tiny to have even a half-integer address. The sliver of a space houses The Silversmith, owned by Ruth Kuzub, a lively Village old-timer who was once famous as one of the Copacabana cabaret dancers, and who now sells costume jewelry as well as some of her own silver creations. Ruth is an animal lover and a self-proclaimed "crazy cat lady." My two dogs adore her and the two cats she keeps there, even though, like most cats, they can't stand dogs. We go there every day—my dogs for the treats Ruth hands out to any canine passersby (and on the off chance the felines will have a change of heart) and I for the stories. It was from one of her employees, an old salt with whom I like to talk about fishing, that I heard this tale.

In the '70s, two brothers from New Jersey opened an Italian restaurant called Sandolino's in the Annisa space. The name in Italian meant "little rowboat" and thus there was a small model scull in the large bay window in front. The brothers' credentials? One had been a waiter, and the other liked to eat. According to popular lore of the time, the older one had a criminal record, so they were only able to get a wine and beer license. From the outset, there were problems. The water heater they installed couldn't produce enough, so they placed a gas burner under the pot sink to heat the water. It was probably not legal then, and it is certainly illegal now. Customers curious about the new restaurant came in the beginning, but the food was so bad it became legendary. The brothers were using their mother's recipes—either she was a terrible cook or a terrible recipe writer. More likely, the chef had no talent. And while there were several kinds of overcooked pasta to choose from, there were only three sauces: an unpalatable red sauce, said red sauce "with meat," and a butter sauce made by throwing a pat of frozen butter on the limp pasta. If customers asked about the little crystals on top, the waiter would lie and call the ice crystals "salt."

Needless to say, after a few months of operation, the little ship was taking on water.

A bilge pump came in the form of a breakfast cook with a local following. He had been the chef at a small counter that was closing in the neighborhood, so the brothers asked him to come cook breakfast and lunch at their place during the day. They would keep the restaurant the same at night. Almost immediately, the restaurant was full, but only when he was cooking. So eventually, they gave up on the Italian concept and renamed the restaurant Sandolino's Deli Café, offering the breakfast cook's menu 23 hours a day. The food was simple but well made—eggs, sandwiches, and coffee, plus beer and wine at good prices. The deli café was one of the first places in the city to have a beer list. People from all walks of life came (as well as the now famous Bill Murray) and for a while it seemed as if it would all be smooth sailing. But old habits die hard, and the brothers were shady with the building's water and electricity and eventually they lost their lease.

By this time, the brothers were rich, and moved Sandolino's around the corner to 9 Jones Street. They kept the name and chef, but made the place glitzy. The bar had big brass lions protruding from each end. There were crystal light fixtures and red and gold everywhere. It was the Russian Tea Room of deli cafés. And they thought it would be charming to play with the menu. A tuna salad sandwich was called the "Ike and Tina Tuna." And the chopped liver? "Gay Liveration." People either took one look inside and walked away, or read the menu and then walked away. The restaurant's identity crisis was too much for her to stay afloat, and the little boat sank for good.

But she lives on in the sea chantey sung by the sales clerk at 184¾ —a small boat, a tiny store, but a tall tale.

PETER LONGO

My mother, Rose, grew up at 190 Bleecker

Street. My father, Angelo, grew up at 201 Bleecker. So you might say she was the girl next door. He, the youngest son of the local baker, and she, the daughter of a piece tailor, met at the Bethlehem Chapel, a social center at 196 Bleecker. He fell like a ton of bricks. His parents and older sisters weren't so sure they wanted the baby of the family to be so involved. Her parents would have nothing of it and sent her away for the summer to stay with a nice couple who had a beautiful place in the country.

Well, Angelo would not be dissuaded. He wrote letter after letter, all very heartfelt and romantic, almost every day. Some were newsy, full of stories about what he was experiencing at home and in the bakery. But they always ended with how much he missed her and how wonderful their life would be together.

They did marry, in the 1930s, and had three children, all raised at 201 Bleecker, the building that Angelo's father had bought in 1905. Rose went to work at *Forbes Magazine*, on Fifth Avenue at 12th Street. My mother would walk home, and I remember her picking me up from the kindergarten at the Children's Aid Society dressed in an Italian knit suit and high heels. She looked great. She never wore flats. Can you imagine that?

In 1960, my parents bought Porto Rico Importing Co., which was started in 1907 by Patsy Albanese at 194 Bleecker. He specialized in food "from the other side," but also had coffee from Puerto Rico, which was highly prized at the time. The pope drank it. "Porto" is the Italian spelling, which my parents kept. They were always behind the register and were very personable. People were traveling then, especially the bohemians, so if a customer asked about beans from some faraway place, they would import them, and the range of coffee expanded.

In the 1970s they decided to retire, so I took over the business. And when the rent went up to $600 a month, I moved the shop to 201 Bleecker, sharing the ground floor with Longo's Sanitary Bakery, still run by the family. Eventually the bakers retired, and I took over their space and started buying the building piece by

Rose Longo and her daughter Mary Elizabeth in front of the
Longo family bakery on Bleecker Street. 1944.

piece. All my uncles and aunts had shares, and it took me twenty-five years to get
permission from each of them, using a formula for buy-outs set up by my grand-
mother, a woman who thought ahead.

My father died in 1978, but Rose continued to live at 201 Bleecker. She was
there for almost eighty years. She mentored generations of the kids who worked
behind the counter. She would hold big dinners for the staff, making a *bagna cauda*,
a kind of Italian fondue, and some of these parties became quite wild. As she got
older she'd spend every day outside on the bench, relaxing with a cup of coffee
and enjoying the company of staff, customers, and friends as they passed by. She
is gone now but she lives on in me. I have only been at 201 Bleecker for sixty-one
years. I hope I catch up.

JESSE MALIN

I grew up in a one-bedroom apartment

with my mom and my younger sister Juliet in Queens, where people lived in their own little bubbles and rarely ventured into the city. I fell in love with rock and roll at a young age, and I especially liked a band called Kiss. Their loud guitars, fire, and makeup spoke to my pre-teenage angst. The other kids hated Kiss and would yell out, "KISS SUCKS." I would get into fights with fans of Led Zeppelin, Black Sabbath, and believe it or not, even The Grateful Dead. After seeing The Sex Pistols on television, I had to start a punk band of my own. If liking Kiss got you beaten up by other rockers, being a punk got you beaten up by everybody.

When the Ramones film *Rock 'n' Roll High School* premiered at the 8th Street Playhouse, I HAD to see it, so I put on my vinyl motorcycle jacket and snuck my twelve-year-old ass into Manhattan. I got out of the subway at Broadway and 8th Street and headed to the theater in the wrong direction, ending up at St. Marks Place. Surrounded by punks, Rastas, hippies, and rockers, I felt I had found my tribe. There was something exciting and dangerous about the area, especially as I walked farther east toward Avenue A. Amongst the swagger and the soul, there was a hardness and desperation that I had never seen before. It was clear that I was going the wrong way. I made a mental note to return very soon.

I made frequent trips back to St. Marks Place, returning home with fanzines, imported records, and cool clothes to share with friends from my band. Other kids would see me getting off the bus with pink Trash and Vaudeville bags and would yell in mocking voices, "Where you coming from . . . The Village?" insinuating that I'd been hanging out on Christopher Street with the cowboys and Indians from The Village People singing "Macho Man" (which might have been fun, too).

One afternoon I called CBGB's from my public school payphone and booked an audition for my new band, Heart Attack. There was no age minimum and the only criterion was that you had to play all original music. The booker told us that punk was dead and that we should look into some new sounds like Rockabilly, Power Pop, and believe it or not, New Romantic. Disillusioned, but still craving something loud and raw, we headed toward Tompkins Square Park, noticing flyers pasted over the walls for bands like The Stimulators and Bad Brains. We suddenly realized we weren't alone in this. We began speeding up our tempos and hanging out in front of an after-hours club called A7.

A new movement was happening with a DIY ethos and uncompromising sound. It was faster, louder, and nastier than anything before: it was called HARDCORE. Heart Attack (now a trio due to some distrusting parents) put out the first NYC hardcore 7-inch record on fanzine label Damaged Goods and we began to tour North America, much to the dismay of my junior high school principal.

After one too many 6 a.m. train rides home from the A7 club, I decided to move into my rehearsal studio at 162 Avenue B. I slept on a foldout lawn chair, lived on outdated yogurts, and busked on the L line to pay the rent. Hip-hop kids were coming out of the projects, graffiti artists were on the street, and there were drag queens down in the park. The low rents allowed everyone a place to create and express themselves, or just really get fucked up.

Eventually Heart Attack broke up in a fire of politically correct judgment—we had become the hierarchy we were fighting. In the summer of 1991, I formed a new band, D Generation, and things began to get exciting again. We ended up in *The New York Times* with a photo of us standing on St. Marks Place. Our first major record deal was signed with the lawyers and CEOs of EMI Records in the dirty, pissed-up bathroom of our local haunt, The Continental. I used some of my advance to open a bar called Coney Island High at 15 St. Marks Place. Once again we were living our dreams without ever going above 14th Street, except for the occasional tour or the night we played Madison Square Garden, opening for Kiss. After that show, I got arrested for having an open container. I tried to tell the cops that I was a native New Yorker and had waited my whole life to play the Garden, but it didn't matter. I spent two days in the Tombs.

I think about the cycles a city goes through historically. People come and go; neighborhoods are built up, broken down, and reborn to find their place in time again. The streets walked by Emma Goldman, Bob Dylan, Charlie Parker, Diane Arbus, Allen Ginsberg, and Joey Ramone are the same streets my grandfather traveled from his tenement apartment to his high school to hear Albert Einstein speak. Even through all these changes, you can still find the art, the beauty, and even some trouble on these East Village streets. The sun still rises over Tompkins Square Park shedding light on a spray-painted wall that reads "The Future is Unwritten."

WYNTON MARSALIS

In 1981 I lived in the Village with my brother

Branford. We had an apartment on Bleecker Street near Broadway. We must have been eighteen and nineteen years old then. Art Blakey lived there, too, and he got us into the building. I remember we used to leave the apartment at twelve o'clock at night and go to all of the clubs in the Village. We would go to the Tin Palace, the Village Vanguard, the Village Gate, and Sweet Basil. I played a lot at a place called Seventh Avenue South, too. And then, we would go to get us some breakfast at Sandolino's around 5 a.m. and come home about 6:30 in the morning. We called that "doing the circuit," doing all the clubs like that in one night. I remember all the musicians and gigs down here in the Village. It was very colorful—it reminded me a lot of the French Quarter of New Orleans. It was much more integrated than the rest of New York City, with a lot of different people, no judgment, and a lot of freedom.

Wynton Marsalis at the Village Vanguard (detail). Photo by Jack Vartoogian/Getty Images. 1993.

GEORGE MATTESON

In what passed as normal for me in about

1980, I was standing on the foredeck of an aging tugboat, an overnight bag at my feet stuffed with three weeks' worth of dirty then redirtied clothing. Having just been paid off up in the pilothouse I carried a couple of thousand dollars rolled up in the top pocket of my flannel shirt. It was February, cold, 2 a.m. and the tug was running light up the Hudson River to drop me off within walking distance of where I lived in Lower Manhattan. There was a good deal of ice in the river and the tug would lurch and rumble when it hit the bigger chunks. The captain made no effort to avoid them.

The city lights, the towers, and the streets were all bright, even at this hour, with business and traffic, but the river was somber as if cut off from the metropolis. And indeed it was, for all along the river bank hung a darkness complicated by jagged structures: first, the West Side Highway still elevated at that time but impossibly decayed, then the cobbled apron beneath the highway through which a dismal bypass wandered, bounded on either side by cyclone fence and a gulag of long termed cars and tractor trailers. Jutting out from shore were ruined docks. Some collapsed, some still fitted with their barnlike cargo sheds, and most stripped flat, decked over with concrete and repurposed as parking lots. Nowhere in all the riverfront from the Trade Center to the foot of Gansevoort Street was there a sign of life.

New York had turned its back on the river. All of the shipping had moved off to Ports Elizabeth and Newark and the city government had begun a long process of making the once vast waterfront establishment of Manhattan disappear. First, they let all leases on marine business expire, then tore down the pier sheds and re-leased the decks for parking. Then in a move both practical and symbolic, they removed all of the cleats and bollards from the docks so that no vessel could ever moor to them again. Then, in a very few years, hurried along by a series of fires and spectacular

From the Barge. Painting by Adele Ursone. 2008.

collapses, most of the remaining structures vanished except for orderly fields of piling stubs marking where the piers had been.

Slowly but steadily the waterfront has since evolved into a splendid but, for me, meaningless park. I go with my dog to the dog run down by Pier 40, I look for winter ducks among the piling stubs: geese, brant, bufflehead, and the occasional coot. In early March there used to be canvasbacks but these don't seem to come anymore.

I remember a long departed friend, an engineer on Liberty ships all through the Second War. One of the last of these ships, the JOHN W. BROWN, once berthed at Pier 42 serving as a marine vocational high school. Deep down in the ship's engine room my friend once acted out a fearful day in winter North Atlantic convoy when his ship had collided with another and he and his engine gang had watched in dream-like horror as the steel side of their ship buckled, then tore, while the bow of the other ripped into the space above their heads, bringing the deadly, icy ocean with it.

Like a cat again, in pantomime the old man moved from valve to pump to manifold giving orders to his mates and orchestrating the desperate race to heel the ship so that the deadly gash might tip above the waterline. The old JOHN W. BROWN, the quiet engines, empty tanks and holds, my friend, and I came briefly back alive in the telling of the story. Today, my friend and almost every other story-teller of New York's maritime past is gone.

But that wintry night the tug headed toward the only spot on that whole stretch of river where even a vestige of the harbor life remained. And this was a lone fire hydrant located just behind the seawall south of Pier 40. That bit of ordinary municipal furniture was one of the few remaining marine watering stations where tugs had been permitted to water up throughout most of the 19th and 20th centuries. Located next to Pier 40, which had been built in 1963 for the use of the Holland America Line of steamships, this station had remained active long after most of the others scattered around the harbor had been shut down and it continued to flow for a few years even after Holland America moved out in the mid-'70s. While all of the other slips along the waterfront had inexorably silted in to wading depth at low tide, the space along the south side of 40 had remained navigable due to the regular passage of tugs gliding up to the hydrant to take on water.

We turned into that slip. Another boat must have visited earlier in the night because the ice which would normally have frozen up thick and solid in there was loose and allowed us to glide through with a diminishing crackle and hiss until we kissed up against the seawall. The captain then edged the engine just barely into clutch to hold the tug's bow against the wall while I disembarked. There was a high bank of snow plowed up against river edge, piled up almost to the height of the tug's bow fender where I stood a moment to plan my leap down to the plowed out street below. I took into account the police car cooping next to the snowbank with a plume of steamy exhaust drifting from its tailpipe. Its headlights were on which I was thankful for as it illuminated the spot where I would have to land. Just in front of the car and right below my perch there was a long black object laid out upon the hard packed snow.

"Watch your step gettin off," the captain called down from the pilothouse window half opened against the cold.

I waved to acknowledge his concern, I jumped carefully but slipped anyway on the icy snowbank and regained my balance only after planting my foot squarely on the black mystery. It gave under my weight like a big squirrel. The police car squawked and the window rolled down.

"Hey, whadda ya' doin'?" the cop demanded.

"Just going home to bed," I replied. Walking backward to examine the thing I had just violated; wondering if it had been fished out of the river or had maybe died crawling toward it.

"Get home safe," he said.

Alphabet City. Photo by Dona Ann McAdams. 1986.

DONA ANN McADAMS

I came to the East Village for the first time

to see Meredith Monk perform at St. Mark's Church. It was 1978, and afterward a few of us decamped to Veselka, a block away on 9th Street at Second Avenue. We went for the soup. Pea soup.

Soon after, I moved to 9th Street, a few doors down from Veselka. My studio was across the street at PS 122—9th Street and First Avenue. A block away from pea soup. Whenever I left the city, for a day job or overnight or a protest in Washington, my reward upon returning was dinner at Veselka. Sometimes a tuna on rye. A hot tea. Borscht maybe. But more often: pea soup.

For the next three decades I lived on 9th Street; I became the house photographer at PS 122 in 1983. This meant documenting every dance and performance that took place in the theater there. I shot black-and-white film with a Leica M3. After a show, the performers often walked down the block to Veselka where they'd sit at a table or the counter and eat pierogi or potato pancakes . . . or a bowl of pea soup.

But my job wasn't done until later. I had to process the film upstairs in my darkroom. I had to make prints to be used for reviews in the *New York Times* or the *Village Voice* the next day. Sometimes this meant staying up late into the night, waiting for the film to dry and then readying the final prints with a hair dryer while a bike messenger waited to pedal them up to the *Times* Culture Desk on 43rd Street. This meant, early in the morning, after a performance, after the prints were safely on their way, there was always Veselka to look forward to, and a bowl of pea soup.

CAROLYN CAPSTICK MEEHAN

It was spring 1981, and I'd leased a vacant store on Hudson Street near Jane Street. With the help of two large sons and one small daughter, I'd just started scraping the layers of old paint off the front when neighbors began attaching friendly notes to the door. I felt welcome from the beginning, despite the occasional "A kids' store? What a strange idea—there are no children in the Village." I ran the shop, called Peanutbutter & Jane, for twenty-seven years.

Two doors north on Hudson, at the corner of Jane, was the No Name Bar. This establishment had many daytime regulars, and one morning just after I'd opened, one of them wandered in, took a long look at the bins of small toys—a wind-up nose that ran around on feet, an entire animal farm in one tiny box, fish pens, drinking straws in the shape of spectacles—and ran back out. Minutes later he returned with three other men to select a variety of toys. Having discovered a cheerfully foolish way to break the monotony of a long day's journey into night on a Village barstool, the No Name regulars dropped by often and became increasingly vocal in their opinions of my inventory.

One morning, a burst of horrific screams emanated from the direction of the No Name, and Natalie, my sales assistant, ran to investigate. She discovered Danny Lettieri, the bar's robust proprietor, holding a case of Guinness Stout and bellowing at full throttle, wedged in the doorway of the bar. In a pool of blood on the sidewalk lay a small finger, a pinkie severed from Danny's hand by the thrust of the heavy case against the doorjamb as he tried to squeeze through. Natalie convinced him to set down the Guinness and then, calmly removing her scarf, tied off his hand with it to stop the bleeding. She then snatched up the pinkie and ran pell-mell behind the bar to immerse it in a glass of milk. After which she called St. Vincent's Hospital for an ambulance.

The doctors at St. Vincent's sprang into action, assembling a team of specialists in microsurgery to save the finger. They knew of Danny because of his kindness

The Cardplayers, on Horatio Street. Photo by Ruth Orkin. 1947.

to Genevieve Camlin, a recently deceased resident of the Village Nursing Home on Hudson at 12th Street, where they had many patients.

Danny first met Genevieve on a snowy afternoon in 1970, when the Belfast-born lady, then a mere eighty-seven years old, walked the block from the nursing home to the No Name. She ordered a Guinness and loudly recited Irish poetry for much of the afternoon. Danny was so enchanted that when she told him to start a tab, he agreed. From that day forward, for an entire decade, she came every day, rain or snow, running up a tab of $10,462.00.

Softhearted Danny had forgiven the debt (though he said he'd never have let her run up the tab if he'd known she'd live so long), and in return for his benevolence the doctors reattached his pinkie for free. It was necessary, however, to lop off its tip and temporarily attach it to the palm of his hand to assure blood flow through the reattached finger.

Danny was tremendously proud of the resulting configuration, and when things were slow at the bar he would wander into Peanutbutter & Jane to show his hand to shoppers, grown-up or not. "Wanna see something?" he'd ask, and carefully lift the bandage to show skin still purple from surgery and the very pink fingertip embedded in his palm. Small children would either scream or ask to touch it, while parents gasped and looked at me for an explanation. Danny would then return to his bar to regale the crowd with how he'd just scared the living daylights out of the folks at Peanutbutter & Jane.

THOMAS MEEHAN

Years ago, in the summer of 1955, when

I first came to New York, I lived in a twenty-five-dollar-a-week room in a rundown old boarding house on Horatio Street. I chose to take up residence in Greenwich Village partly because I'd always lived in a village—a tiny one of around 2,500 residents in Upstate New York, apple-knocker country—but also partly because I'd often read and heard about the Village's long-time reputation as a welcoming haven for aspiring young creative types. And that I certainly was—a cliché of clichés, the fuzzy-minded young man, just out of college, who dreamed of someday becoming a world-famous writer. I wasn't exactly sure what sort of world-famous writer I wanted to be, but I was leaning toward either a revered master of the short story, like Chekhov, or a Nobel Prize–winning novelist, like Hemingway or Faulkner. Either was okay with me.

Once unpacked in my rented room, I set up my portable Olivetti and a ream of typing paper on a rickety table and sat down to turn out a wry but poignant and deeply touching short story that I imagined would soon appear in the pages of *The New Yorker*. But the muse did not turn up that day on Horatio Street, or on any other day that summer or fall. Alone in the city, pretty much penniless, and knowing almost no one in New York, I took to wandering aimlessly all over the Village and Lower Manhattan, gathering material, I told myself, for the torrent of stories and novels I'd soon be spewing forth.

And it was on one of those wanderings, early on a blisteringly hot Sunday afternoon, that I found myself trudging down Christopher Street and coming upon the Theater de Lys, which was playing something called *The Threepenny Opera*— some sort of musical, I assumed. A matinee was just about to start, tickets cost only $3.50, and the theater—as a banner outside proclaimed—was air-conditioned. And so, knowing absolutely nothing about Kurt Weill, Bertolt Brecht, or Weimar Germany, I decided to get out of the pizza-oven heat and kill a couple of hours at *The Threepenny Opera*.

It was, of course, a revelation, mind-bogglingly great, still one of the most thrilling experiences I've ever had in the theater. Weill's music, dissonant and slyly tuneful at the same time, took my breath away, and Brecht's savagely funny libretto and lyrics (as translated by Marc Blitzstein) stunned with their utter brilliance. And then there was the cast, led by Weill's widow, Lotte Lenya herself, bringing down the house with "Pirate Jenny."

I walked out of the Theater de Lys in a daze, little knowing that I had just seen what is now considered to be perhaps the most legendary and ground-breaking theatrical production ever done Off-Broadway. What I did know, however—fifty-nine years ago, on that hot Sunday afternoon—was that someday, somehow, I wanted to be a writer for the theater, the musical theater.

I never did write a novel, and although I later published a number of comic stories in *The New Yorker*, I have in fact mainly made my living writing the books for musicals, and recently, for instance, had three of mine running at the same time on Broadway, none of them admittedly in the same class as *The Threepenny Opera*. Where in the world but Greenwich Village could a young apple-knocker wander into a theater and come upon so remarkable a work that he was inspired to change the course of his life? Nowhere!

Hudson Street Cornices. Painting by Andrew Jones. 2003.

ISAAC MIZRAHI

My mother used to say, "If you want to be

young forever, move to the Village." I arrived more than twenty years ago and have lived here ever since. I will probably move out feet first.

When I was a kid growing up in Brooklyn, the best times for me were trips to the Village. In the car my heart would leap when I saw the light shining like the Emerald City from the mouth of the Brooklyn-Battery Tunnel. On family excursions we would pass the Women's House of Detention on Greenwich Avenue, and my father would point and say, "That's what happens to bad ladies." I thought he meant the Jefferson Market Library next door, and I swear I saw desperate faces and flailing arms reaching out from barred windows in the Gothic tower. The women's jail was torn down in the '70s and the site is now a garden. But to this day, in my mind, the Jefferson Market tower looms on the corner of 10th Street and Sixth Avenue as a warning to young women about the tough consequences of going wrong in the big city.

Jefferson Market Court and 447-461 Sixth Avenue. Photo by Berenice Abbott. 1938. The Women's House of Detention looming in the background was demolished in 1974.

PETER MYERS

I grew up in Keswick, in the Lake District

of England, and in 1971 I worked like a dog at my father's butcher shop to save enough money for a two-week visit to New York.

A friend collected me at JFK and we had a few drinks at his apartment on Horatio Street. Then we went to the Lion's Head, on Christopher Street, where the bartender lifted the hatch to come out and shake my hand. I thought it a very nice gesture. And then we went to another bar called the Bells of Hell, where I fell asleep at a table.

The Bells of Hell was on 13th Street, where Café Loup is now. Because of the name, AT&T refused to list it in the phone book. It comes from an old British Army song that ends a play by Brendan Behan: "the bells of hell go ting-a-ling-a-ling." I soon had a job there, tending bar in the afternoon, making $50 a day. I called my father and said, "I'm not coming back for a while."

The owner was Malachy McCourt, one of four brothers from Ireland. The others were Michael, Alphie, and Frank, who twenty-four years later would write *Angela's Ashes*. In the '70s, Malachy was the more famous brother, an actor with a radio show on WMCA. He used to park Angela, their mother, at the bar some afternoons. We spent hours complaining about the state of American tea.

I worked at the Bells until it closed in 1972. The death knell was a dispute with Con Ed, which cut the electric and gas. We survived by candlelight for less than a month. Then I thought, that's it, back to England and the butcher shop.

A year later I was back in the Village, this time with a bank loan. I saw the Bells still had a For Rent sign. The topic came up that night at the Lion's Head, and within a week I had a partner and a ten-year lease on the place.

I put in a newspaper rack stocked with Sunday papers from the UK. And we had what Keith Richards said was greatest jukebox in New York. English friends would airmail me the UK top 20 singles, and for a quarter you could hear Queen's

"Bohemian Rhapsody" two months before it was released in the States. We had live music, too, on weekends.

The Bells was in friendly competition with the Lion's Head. In fact, that's how I priced the drinks: ten cents less than whatever they were charging. They had the pols and the newspapermen, and we had more of the avant-garde: Lester Bangs, the rock critic, and Douglas Kenney, a founder of *National Lampoon*. One of our bartenders, Nick Browne, had a column in the *Voice* called "A Few Quick Ones."

The '70s was a fun time. One of our greatest nights was the blackout of '77. We used to have candles in those chintzy orange pots on each table. Lo and behold, I'd bought a gross of them the day before. In those days I worked the afternoon shift and would go for a siesta at 6 o'clock. At 9:30 the bartender, "Denver Dave" Coles, rang to ask if he should close up, because all of New York had lost power. "Are you nuts, this is going to be one of the busiest nights of the year," I told him. It was July, very hot, no AC, so we left the front door open. We had all those candles and two magnificent ice machines. We stayed open until 4 o'clock that morning, the place was packed right through the night.

A year later I sold out to my partner—it's a rule with bars that partners will disagree—and six months later there was a problem with Con Ed. The electric bills had never been more than $300 a month, even in summer with the AC going full blast. They discovered the mistake and slapped him for $10,000. Con Ed actually closed down the place twice.

RON PADGETT

Horatio Street

is way over in the West Village
N.Y.C.

In a one-room basement apartment
I'd wake up
Morning? look
out the window
Shoes

The light a sort of pleasant untorn gray
a life made simple
by the absence of weather
which made reading a breeze

Symbols of Transformation

My desk a discard
from a dentist bent
on going modern
and a toaster with faulty wiring that mysteriously got better
and is still my toaster

and James Baldwin who had lived upstairs
until a few weeks ago now a ghost

For local color the local yokel
The White Horse was some drunk people's White House

Gelatinous water slapdashed against West Side piers
with those refrigerated diesel meat trucks
pink in the dawn light
rolling up Horatio at four or five
four or five inches from my interested ear

and late-night rain against the all-nite diner where
giant Men came in in white smocks
smeared with blood dried brown

and the drunken stranger in suit and tie
who chased me down the street
tears streaming down his face
crying "Peter! Peter!"

It was a nice street
not spectacular or pretty
pleasantly remote
pleasantly near
1961–62

IOANNIS PAPPOS

I was part of the cocky Hermès-tie invasion

of the West Village. At the peak of the dot-com craze, I moved to New York and leased a loft on Leroy Street at the Printing House, which was practically a frat house for Wall Streeters. The annual rent could buy a small condo in Texas, but it was spacious. My first night I gave my bike a spin around the living room—I had arrived.

Right away I recognized that the West Village was in the throes of collision. It harbored a mishmash of different species and formed a battleground of sorts for MBAs like me with money (at least on paper) and subletting artists. We had Pastis and Da Silvano, they had El Faro and Tavern on Jane. We all mixed at Florent and rubbed shoulders, literally, at snug La Bonbonniere during hangover Sundays. Dog walkers and tattooed musicians would "Hey, man" me at Meatpacking District parties, and I felt somehow abashed—it was as though they picked up on everything about our white-collar raid and still they pardoned us. I wanted to see them fighting for rent-justice, I expected contempt and dirty looks, but those madcaps didn't seem to give a damn. I envied them. As soon as the 9/11 mourning subsided, the Spotted Pig and six, seven (I've stopped counting) Marc Jacobs stores sealed my hood's fate: being poor and marginal in the West Village was now almost suspicious.

After changing jobs one time too many, I found myself under a corporate non-compete restriction. Still blessed with an expense account—as many were in the mid-'00s—I worked for a year out of Sant Ambroeus restaurant on Perry Street. There in my Birkenstocks, I made the pink marble bar my new kitchen, desk, and living room. Fllanza the barista was my "roommate" and Eddy, the permanent West 4th Street vagrant, my "doorman." Sant Ambroeus regulars, power-lunch money managers, and HBO artists smiled at my bedhead hair and rolled their eyes when I smoked with the AA folks next door. I was getting courteously snubbed. Soon enough, I became lazy and unfit for the corporate grind—my world was

Swimmer, Back Flip. Pier 49, Bank Street. Photo by Shelley Seccombe. 1979.

turning upside down. Out of frustration, one day I yelled "Get a life!" at the tour guide helping tourists take pictures of where *Sex and the City* was shot. That act of West Village disobedience made me start writing.

JAMES STEWART POLSHEK AND ELLYN POLSHEK

Suddenly, in the middle of a dark, moonless

and frigid December night, in 1973, we awoke to a loud and insistent knocking on the front door of our sixth-floor apartment. We leaped out of bed and rushed to the door to find the young daughter of a neighbor shouting "Fire, fire!" as she ran off to wake others. We quickly gathered our teenage children, Peter and Jenny, and our grown-up English guest, Philip, who was still sleeping. The kitchen was already filled with smoke and the back door was too hot to touch. With our beagle, Pooch, and our Yugoslav turtle, Mali Ston, we ran for the front door. As we hurried down the stairs, unaware that we would never live there again, firemen raced past us on their way up.

West 9th Street was already blocked off with fire trucks, a Red Cross van, and a cluster of reporters. Within minutes we were horrified to see flames shooting from the roof, only a few feet above the ceiling of our apartment. It was barely eleven degrees above zero and we were dressed only in coats or blankets over our pajamas and whatever footwear we could grab—standing there dazed by this frightful intrusion into our ordinary lives.

Many hours later, accompanied by a fireman, we returned to inspect the damage and recover valuables and some clothes. Portions of our floor had sagged into the apartment below. The rear of the apartment was virtually destroyed. The refrigerator had melted. Our son's Lionel trains—a gift from his grandfather—and our daughter's beloved books were gone. A painting was now a blank canvas with the colorful oils in a pool at its base. Only Snoopy, Jenny's beloved stuffed animal, now smoky and singed, survived. And of course so did we.

Some days later we learned the apparent cause of the conflagration. A high school student on the second floor had disobeyed his parents' admonition not to use the fireplace. In order to hide his misfeasance, he waited until the ashes could be disposed of in the dumbwaiter that carried trash to the cellar. Alas, a few unanticipated glowing embers remained below the gray ash and were unleashed by the updraft in the chimney-like void, ballooning into a four-alarm fire.

Our building, 42 West 9th Street, constructed in 1882, was one of three designed by the architect Ralph S. Townsend. Its name—Portsmouth—is proudly carved into the brownstone of the portico over the stoop. The unorthodox Queen Anne style celebrates the remarkable variety of architecture in Greenwich Village. And the six-story skip-stop elevator is the most imaginative aspect of the architecture.

By the time the Portsmouth was restored, we had moved to a new nest on Washington Square West. It is tempting to end this story with "and we never looked back." But we did. From our north-facing windows we can still see the rear facade of where we once lived.

Blimp Above New York. Painting by Peter Ruta. 1989.

LOU
REED

My favorite moments in the Village are

always with the beautiful sun drifting over the Hudson River. And as I look out,
I am taking photos in my mind or with one of my cameras. It's always great for
me to start the day with a beautiful photo and then three hours of tai chi, all these
golden moments in the Village.

MARK RUSSELL

PS 122 had a doorman when I first started

working there in the early '80s. He was a cordial, reasonably well-dressed gentleman who stood in the small, protected entrance to the center. I would greet him and he would just nod. He kept a keen eye on the street, in both directions, and worked long hours. Of course he was not our doorman. He was supervising the drug sales that made the corner of First Avenue and Ninth Street a very popular destination.

A team of three individuals seemed to work for our doorman. Constantly walking up and down the block on First Avenue, yelling at one another occasionally, getting into little fights and spats, mostly looking furtive. They were skinny-wired hustlers, two women and a man, with a very intense business life. They kept way longer hours than I did, and this was quite an accomplishment since I was practically the only full-time employee of an active arts center. PS 122 was busy with performances, classes, rehearsals, and community meetings all hours of the day, seven days a week. I would wave hi to them in the morning and then sometimes after 1 a.m. when I left, we would nod goodnight. We were just fellow working stiffs in the East Village. We never spoke.

I had a theory that the police precinct let the trade flourish on our corner because they did not want the newbie NYU kids headed any farther into Alphabet City. They could keep an eye on the situation from First Avenue more easily. The pot trade (I think it was mostly weed at our location) went on unencumbered. Once in a while there would be a little street bust—on one occasion the police discovered the substance in question hidden in a baby stroller. Sometimes a rookie cop would come by and ask us if he could watch the corner from our windows, and we would

Mary Help of Christians R. C. Church, on East 12th Street. Photo by
Allen Ginsberg. 1985. Despite community protest, the church
was demolished in 2013.

let him, explaining the activity below. The rookies would watch, take notes, and leave, but rarely return. Nothing changed.

This was before the crack epidemic really hit the East Village. Before the building across the street had to physically evict the super because he had become a tool for dealers who had moved into his apartment. Before the SWAT teams shut down East 10th Street one day and discovered a whole series of buildings connected through their walls for the drug runners. This was before a storefront gallery owner closed up and left because a body came crashing through his back roof.

By then our doorman was long gone. He just disappeared one day. It was said he had a pistol on him the whole time he worked our doorway. In many ways those were safer days than the ones that came later. We would miss that brief time when PS 122 was a doorman building.

Backyard Gardens, East Village. Photo by Allen Ginsberg. 1984.

At the New York Studio School. Photo by Daniel Gerdes. 2008.

JOOP SANDERS

In the 1940s, a group of Village artists met almost every night to discuss art and politics. In good weather, we met on the northwest corner of Washington Square Park near the "hanging tree," which was huge because it was fed by Minetta Brook. If nobody was there, the crowd would be around the corner at the Waldorf Cafeteria on the east side of Sixth Avenue near the corner of 8th Street. The regulars were Bill de Kooning, Philip Pavia, Milton Resnick (after the war), Ahron Ben-Shmuel, Conrad Marca-Relli, Franz Kline, Landes Lewitin, Ibram Lassaw, Max Schnitzler, Earl Kirkham, and me, and occasionally Aristodimos Kaldis and Charlie Egan and others. The owners of the Waldorf would try to throw us out some of the time because we sat there all night and most of us never bought food because we didn't have any money. We talked from ten to midnight when they closed. Eventually, the Waldorf owners threw us out completely, and that is why our artist's club was founded in 1949 on the initiative of Philip Pavia. The Club rented a place on 8th Street between University Place and Broadway where we could meet, hold discussions, and drink, on Thursday nights only—except for special occasions like my own wedding party (for which the walls were decorated by Elaine de Kooning and Ernestine Lassaw). A few of the members finally started making money from their art. When they were through drinking and talking at the Club, they would head to the Cedar Tavern to continue into the night. Some of the more abstinent members repaired to the Chuck Wagon, a coffee shop on the corner of University Place and 8th Street diagonally across the street from the Cedar Bar. There was a lot of traffic back and forth between the Chuck Wagon and the Cedar Bar.

MARTICA SAWIN

A glimpse through the iron gate into the

shaded courtyard of Patchin Place is for me the quintessential image of Greenwich Village, recollected from childhood sleepovers with a widowed friend of my mother who lived there in a thirty-dollar-a-month walk-up. For a nine-year-old from the suburbs to arrive in the Village atop a double-decker Fifth Avenue bus was already a novelty, but even more exotic were my visits to the slightly askew brick house at the end of the courtyard. My hostess was a genteel Southern lady, living frugally on an Army widow's pension. Her apartment consisted of a small, low-ceilinged sitting room with an inoperable fireplace and a bedroom that barely accommodated a single bed; the "kitchen" was a closet with a hotplate. E. E. Cummings, a Patchin Place neighbor, sometimes dropped in for afternoon tea. Since tea required cupcakes I would be allowed to go out the gate to the bakery down the block on 10th Street and select what I thought would please a poet. The forbidding Women's House of Detention cast a solemn shadow on the neighborhood, but just around the corner on 11th Street was the leafy oasis of the Rhinelander Gardens.

Designed by James Renwick and built in 1854, the block of connected row houses had a facade fronted by two stories of iron grillwork, giving it the look of a transplant from New Orleans's Garden District. Sitting on the steps leading to its long verandah, secluded from the street by the portico's hanging vines, one could enjoy a cool retreat from the hot asphalt on a summer day. Later when I lived in the city, I kept expecting to round a corner and come upon that gracious residential row until it dawned on me that the modern, no-frills P.S. 41 stood precisely on the site. The Rhinelander Gardens had fallen victim to the over-active wrecking ball of the 1950s.

These visits also introduced me to my first art exhibition, in the form of an array of paintings, prints, and drawings hung on the fences of the townhouses surrounding Washington Square. Among those who later achieved international fame was Franz Kline, who showed his early work of thickly painted landscapes on the grillwork of a wrought iron fence.

The City in Pink and Gray, from Fifth Avenue and 12th Street. Painting by Jane Freilicher. 2006.

Fourth Avenue Book Row. Circa 1940s.

MIMI SHERATON

The most evocative location for me in Greenwich Village is 9th Street and Fifth Avenue, just a few steps from the one-room basement apartment I moved into early in the fall of 1945, my junior year at NYU. At that corner I always experience a mental flashback to the scene and activities that beguiled me as I began what was to become an extended stay in the Village—sixty-nine years and still counting.

Although new as a resident, I had spent more of my first two years at college exploring the Village than I did studying and was already captivated by what seemed to a girl from Flatbush like raffish, offbeat charms. The scene I recall at 9th and Fifth includes the jaunty red double-decker Fifth Avenue buses; the plant-trimmed sidewalk café of the Fifth Avenue Hotel, where a lavish Sunday brunch buffet cost a whopping $1.25; the graceful Rhinelander apartments on the west side of the avenue between 8th Street and Washington Square Park; the Brevoort Hotel; and, just to the north, a few red-brick townhouses, one of which, on the southeast corner, held a plaque saying Mark Twain had lived there. That same plaque is now mounted on the north side of 11 Fifth Avenue, the Brevoort high-rise apartment house.

On January 12, 1946, I sat on the steps of that brownstone watching segments of the World War II Victory Parade proceed up Fifth Avenue, honoring our victory and the Eighty-Second and Thirteenth Airborne Divisions that had contributed to it. With the war so recently over, many had not yet returned, and the Village had a sort of quiet, expectant air, as though something great was about to happen.

It was a neighborhood of artists, writers, bohemians, and celebrities of all sorts, including the poets E. E. Cummings and W. H. Auden, and Eleanor Roosevelt, who lived on Washington Square Park and picked up Sunday papers on 8th Street as she walked the presidential black Scottish terrier, Fala. It seemed a peaceful almost exurban village. One of my main delights was to spend Sunday morning sitting in what we called the Circle, the fountain pool just behind the Arch. Often not filled with water until midday—if at all—it provided a convivial neighborhood gathering place. Equipped with the *New York Times*, the *Herald-Tribune*, and sketchpads, we spent the morning there waiting for folk singers to gather. The most memorable for me was the lovely Susan Reed with her flowing copper hair and lyrical voice and guitar.

One revelation was contemporary art, something I had not seen or understood until I began frequenting the Whitney Museum on West 8th Street and where I was first struck by the works of Jacob Lawrence. Shopping meant artisanal jewelry shops, Fred Leighton's Mexican wares, and the cozy interior with fireplace and Christmas glögg at the Washington Square Book Shop, also on 8th Street.

Always interested in food and restaurants, my friends and I saved for meals at Sea Fare on 8th Street, sturgeon and goose liverwurst at Davis's (officially the 8th Street Delicatessen), the Brevoort restaurant and once, only once, the legendary Lafayette on 9th Street and University Place. For Italian food it was "Mother" Bertolotti's or Eddie's Aurora on 4th Street. We skimped at Chock full o'Nuts on University Place, the Waldorf Cafeteria on Sixth Avenue (not yet Avenue of the Americas and still not to me), or across that avenue to the lively Jefferson Diner. And for Friday night college gatherings, it was Ed Winston's Tropical Bar at East 8th, near University Place. The drinking age in those days was eighteen, and we certainly made the most of that indulgence. How lovely it would be to go one more round of chug-a-lugging at that palmy oasis.

Greenwich Village map (detail) by Tony Sarg. 1934.

A MAP
of
GREENWICH VILLAGE
by TONY SARG

...n's Store on Union Square,   6. Alice McCollister Restaurant
...now's Restaurant. 14th St.   7. Eighth Street Playhouse·
...hambeau Rest. and Bar   8. Whitney Museum of Am Art.
...rles Restaurant·   9. Bertolotti's Night Club·
...mont Restaurant·   10. El Gaucho Rest.

West 11th Street Stoops. Painting by Andrew Jones. 1999.

BROOKE SHIELDS

I am a native New Yorker. I was born and
raised on the Upper East Side and spent thirty years living in a townhouse. I had no
intention of ever leaving and viewed downtown as a different city, another world
altogether.

After 9/11, my husband and I felt drawn to Lower Manhattan. We wanted to
help in the rebirth of our city. We began a house hunt, searching from Chelsea to
Battery Park. None of the renovated properties we saw appealed to us. We decided
to switch gears and view brownstones that needed work. The moment I walked
into the pre-war, multi-family building in the West Village, I felt like I had returned
home. I saw our future. I instantly saw how my family would spend our days. I pic-
tured my girls running around doing cartwheels, picked the spot for the Christmas
tree, and even decided where I'd drink my morning coffee. Within twenty-four
hours, the place was ours.

We began a four-year renovation. Ripping into the walls, we found a record of
payment rendered to an actress in the early 1900s as well as a candy wrapper from
the '60s. Shortly after moving in, a neighbor dropped a note of welcome into our
mailbox. On the card was a picture of three old ladies in housedresses, with a dog
sitting on a stoop. The photo was from the '50s, and the stoop was our front steps.
There is history here, and people respect it.

The friendliness one encounters in the West Village is unlike that of any other
area in the city. People still make eye contact and are actually interested to hear
how you are doing. There is an Old World warmth you feel from your neighbors
and a sense that they look out for each other. I am thrilled my girls are experiencing
life in a real neighborhood in the middle of such a metropolitan city. I want them
to grow up walking to school and knowing and supporting local shop owners and
restaurant proprietors. We know our mailman! Whenever I describe our neighborhood to people, they think I live in Vermont or Connecticut. Nope, it's the Village,
I say. And I love it.

WILLIAM SOFIELD

Like most New Yorkers I suffer extreme

remorse for the lost city of my youth. Anyone questioning how much the atmosphere of the town has changed over the last thirty-odd years need only revisit *Taxi Driver*. The West Village I trawled was an unnerving collision of the rough and the refined, where leather men and ladies, many painted, lived in happy juxtapose. I lived in a miniature fifth-floor walkup at 96 Perry Street, with one and frequently more roommates. I summered on tar beach, pumped up at the Sheridan Square Gym, and was educated in all things antique in the salons of Niall Smith and Ruth Burke along Bleecker Street. Saturday evenings were usually spent under the protective custody offered by the corroding carcass of the elevated West Side Highway and Sundays were dawdled amidst glass shards in the cathedrals that were the abandoned pier buildings along the Hudson. The West Village was incandescent, smart, and energetically dangerous.

In the autumn of 1983 I curated an exhibition for the Whitney titled Metamanhattan that included Steven Holl's "Bridge of Houses," a proposal for the reuse and rehabilitation of a section of the elevated railway line paralleling Washington Street. Also included in the show was Lorna Dune's "Do Not Drive In," a project in which abandoned cars were towed to a pier so that pedestrians might enjoy a movie on a large screen with river views. A few years later, I nearly killed my mother with change-of-address cards announcing my move to 12 Gay Street, a Federal townhouse once a speakeasy and part-time residence of mayor Jimmy Walker. A few years after that, I could be found at 380 West 12th Street, a cold-storage warehouse converted to lofts across from the Gulf Coast restaurant and beneath the magnificent gilded sign of Superior Ink. I kept offices above a slaughterhouse on West 14th Street and ate three meals a day at the newly opened Florent on Gansevoort Street. Florent had the advantage of being open twenty-four hours, which neatly coincided with my work and play schedules. The Mineshaft, L.U.R.E., Hellfire, Anvil, J's, Jackie 60, White Horse Tavern, West World, Spike, Hogs & Heifers, along with clubs and

Rotterdam Passing Pier 51. Photo by Shelley Seccombe. 1978.

theaters too numerous to mention, provided nightly amusement. With characteristically circular New York irony, the concrete lip balcony of my loft looked onto the very section of elevated railway included in my Whitney show. In an annual ritual I dubbed Prophylaxis, a performance for the prevention of demolition, I invited neighbors overlooking the deserted railway to fill Fourex condoms—used because they were made of lambskin—with moist soil and wildflower seeds and wing them onto the tracks below. We enjoyed lavish blooms all summer.

That particular stretch of what was later to become the High Line is long gone, along with many of my old haunts, victims of the economic and cultural devastation in the wake of the AIDS crisis that hit the West Village hard. Truth be told, I don't miss the smell of rotten beef at dawn, urine-soaked alleys, or the occasional muggings. I do enjoy with enthusiasm my new sport of watching tipsy girls in couture navigate cobbled streets in stilettos after an evening of fine dining in former sex clubs. Neighbors continue to restore magnificent Italianate townhouses that line streets with simple first names, and I am seeing the benefits of Plant It on Perry thirty years after I first volunteered to push seedlings into dirt the consistency of concrete under the watchful wand of Rollerina. I fancy that my little grassroots condom-slinging each spring might have contributed to the creation and protection of the High Line, and I encourage others to be judicious in preserving whatever remnants of our neighborhood's rougher industrial past that remain.

RAYMOND SOKOLOV

In the early '70s, when I was reviewing restaurants for the *Times*, I successfully resisted the temptation to claim that in the course of dining out for the newspaper, I had caught sight of the notoriously reclusive Howard Hughes, wolfing down a soufflé at Lutece or sending back a pizza at John's. But in 1974, after I had left the paper and it was too late to let inquiring minds know, I actually did think I saw Hughes sharing a beer with an elderly blonde, her face hidden behind a veil, at a table next to the fireplace at Chumley's.

The former Bedford Street speakeasy was crowded with college students too focused on each other, or perhaps too young, to recognize Hughes. I forced myself to get up and squeeze through the crowded room to his table.

"Good evening, Mr. Hughes," I said. "Welcome to the Village."

He looked me in the eye, hesitated, and then said gravely: "Could you get me another beer, son?"

I nodded and walked to the bar. Maybe it wasn't Howard Hughes, I thought. He didn't have Kleenex boxes protecting his feet from microbial contamination.

Decades later, I live down the block from Chumley's, an even shorter walk from a galaxy of much better restaurants—Annisa, Casa, August—but my fondest hope is the reopening of my old haunt, which collapsed during the building's renovation. Reportedly, the original fixtures have been saved along with the tables carved with the initials of real and hopeful Village artists and writers. Their ghosts will hover in the new Chumley's—Mailer, various bohemians named Max, and a big wraith with a mustache, his veiled blonde moll in tow.

ANDREW SOLOMON

When I was a child, I remember driving downtown with my parents to look out the window at the hippies. I think we kept the car doors locked. When I was a little older, we occasionally came to a downtown restaurant called John Clancy's, where we had the most delicious fish ever. My mother took cooking classes with John Clancy, and he would come out from the kitchen to greet us with fanfare. A little later, we'd come south to SoHo to eat at Chanterelle. We used to visit the original Barnes & Noble, back when it was a one-stop store for textbooks. We would go for brunch at the Nom Wah Tea Parlor in Chinatown, or we'd go buy raisin cream cheese at Russ & Daughters on the Lower East Side. I liked downtown, but it was a foreign country to me; I knew numerous European cities better than I did the world below 34th Street.

With the gradual realization that I was gay, I understood that I would have to reckon with Lower Manhattan. In junior high, I used to go downtown secretly, so that I could see gay people, so that I could understand what I might become. The waiters at John Clancy's had a conspiratorial air, happier in their mutuality than I thought gay people were supposed to be. I studied them closely while I ate my bouillabaisse. I would stroll the length of Christopher Street, hiding when anyone tried to talk to me, attempting to understand their unfathomable similarity to me.

Then I grew up. And I had many friends, gay and straight, in Greenwich Village and even in emergent Chelsea. I lived in the UK for most of a decade, and when I settled back in New York, I set up shop on 15th Street and Sixth Avenue, though my mother fretted that the neighborhood was unsafe. I remember someone asked me how it felt to have moved back home, and I said that I hadn't moved back home; I lived in a different place from the one where I grew up.

West 4th Street. Photo by Alexandra Stonehill. 2013.

When it came time to make a permanent decision and buy a house, I bought in the heart of the Village, on what I still think is the prettiest block in town. I had lived in London and I had grown to like vertical living at low altitude better than horizontal apartments way up in the air. But I also felt as though I could keep inventing myself downtown. There was scope for me to be both the adventurer I'd tried to become in England and the anxious schoolboy I had been when I lived on 72nd Street.

I was afraid of the Village when I was little, afraid of those men with long hair and tie-dyed shirts who smoked pot in Washington Square. They felt very alien, and I was worried that their strangeness might prove contagious. In my adolescence, I was terrified of those gay people heading for the docks at night, some of them drag queens, some of them in leather from head to foot; I hoped it wasn't inevitable that I end up like them. But now I have dabbled in everything I once eschewed, and now I have stopped finding difference upsetting, and I have come to prefer sharing the streets with people who haven't grown up all in the same way and in the same place and with the same ambitions. And so now what I mourn is the disappearance of some of the oddness and grunge of the Village; now I'm nostalgic for the way it was when it scared me. But I like the way it's changed, too: it used to feel like the margin of the center of the world, and now it feels like the center of the center of the world. And it's still the prettiest block in New York.

PAUL TAYLOR

There were Hootenannies in Washington

Square Park and Happenings on St. Marks Place during the 1960s, but all was quiet in my corner of the Village. Or so it seemed to me, just a little kid at the time.

My family moved to an apartment at 52 Bank Street, on the corner of West 4th Street, in 1958. When we left, a decade later, I was twelve years old. In my memories of growing up there, I'm always hanging out with friends: walking together to P.S. 41 in the morning; playing stoopball on the street; buying Archie comic books at Andy's (on West 11th and Bleecker, where Bookmarc is now); riding our bikes to Cub Scout meetings in the basement of the First Presbyterian Church on Fifth Avenue; swimming in the Leroy Street pool during the summers.

Most of all, I remember the hours and hours I spent roaming around the neighborhood with the United Lawkeepers of Bank Street, which we referred to as UNLKOBS. Our posse of five or six boys hid messages for one another behind door panels and kept a lookout for mayhem and crimes. We took shortcuts from Bank to West 11th Street by dodging from backyard to backyard through gaps between buildings and unlocked gates. My friend Georgie sometimes had access to a short-wave radio belonging to his father, a captain in the Navy; whenever his dad was at sea we'd bring out the radio and give reports to anyone with a walkie-talkie about what was happening on the block. (Not much.)

My friends and I liked to buy candy bars and cold sodas at the Shanvilla Market, across the street from where I lived. On really hot summer days, the owner—Patrick Mulligan—would sometimes let us cool off in the walk-in freezer. Or we'd scoot over to Bleecker and wait for the iceman, Tom, as he made his delivery rounds to restaurants. We'd reach under the green canvas and chip off pieces of ice; if he saw us, Tom would chase us down the street. Being a lawbreaker was almost as exciting as being a Lawkeeper.

So many of my favorite places are long gone. Exotic Aquatics, which I liked to visit with my friend Arnold when he was buying fish for his tank. Jon Vie Bakery, where my mother bought a dessert every Sunday on our way to dinner at my grand-mother's apartment at 41 Fifth Avenue. Loew's Sheridan Theater (now a triangular park at the intersection of Seventh Avenue and West 12th Street), then one of the great movie palaces in the city, where I'd meet my friends at the weekend matinee for kids, a double feature that lasted four hours!

Did we ever go farther afield? Our small corner of the Village seemed vast at the time, ranging from Bank Street to Washington Square Park. There was just one restriction about places, one rule that could never be broken. I was forbidden by my mother ever to go west of Hudson Street, which was considered very dangerous territory. By the time I was old enough to venture over there, my family had moved out of the Village.

Boy Reading Ha Ha Comic Book. Photo by Morris Engel. 1947.

CALVIN TRILLIN

I don't suppose there is anyone who had
more of a blanket disregard for clubs than my wife Alice, but she always made an
exception for Tiro a Segno, an Italian-American social club on MacDougal Street,
only a few blocks from our house. She did that despite the fact that, since she was
neither male nor Italian, her application for membership would have been subject to an automatic double blackball before anyone even said hello. We began
going there in the late Sixties with our friend Wally Popolizio. Wally was prac-
ticing law in the Village then, in an office called Fazio & Popolizio, sharing with
the American Accordion Association. It was on 8th Street, over the Florsheim
shoe store. What I remember best about the office is that it displayed a wooden
model of the cart Wally's father used to deliver coal and ice after the Popolizios
immigrated to Leroy Street from Basilicata, in the boot of Italy, around the turn
of the century.

Wally had been active in the political battles between the regulars and the
reformers in the Village—even though he had the personality of a regular, he was
with the reformers—and he spent some time as the head of Community Planning
Board Number Two. He was later, at one time or another, a partner in a Wall Street
law firm with a name like Thatcher Baxter Hatcher (a firm Wally and I both referred
to as "the goyim") and chairman of the New York City Housing Authority. The
wooden model of the ice cart accompanied him wherever he went. I met Wally
on what he would have called "a real estate matter"—someone had recommended
him as a lawyer who could provide guidance around the pitfalls involved in buying
a place to live in the Village—and once the matter had been disposed of, he seemed
to add to his other duties the informal responsibility of seeing to it that our family
didn't do anything disastrously foolish. He did not relinquish that responsibility
until his death, in 1992.

Café Figaro (detail), on the corner of MacDougal and Bleecker
Streets. Photo by Robert Otter. 1965.

Wally had a strong sense of family. Once, when I seemed about to entangle myself in some small public contretemps, he phoned to tell me that whatever it was I wanted to say could be said later, when my enemies couldn't use it against me. "And who are your enemies?" he asked, as if conducting a review of examination questions with a particularly slow student.

I had been wondering about the same thing myself. "Enemies?" I said.

"Everybody but your family," he said, and hung up.

Alice loved Wally, but we didn't have to face the question of whether her affection for him would have been strong enough to overcome her feelings about clubs if Tiro a Segno had resembled the sort of place that comes to mind when you think of, say, the Union League Club or the Racquet Club. Tiro, which had been put together out of two Village brownstones, didn't look like an uptown club. The dining room was dominated by a huge mural of the harbor of Naples that had been improved by the addition of some other famous sights of Italy, such as Pompeii and Michelangelo's *David*. The atmosphere was what I think of as New York Italian. I confessed a long time ago that I'm soft on Italians. I meant New York Italians—particularly Lower Manhattan Italians—although it's also true that I often find myself in a sunny frame of mind when I'm in Italy. If I had to face a panel that told me it is out of bounds these days to express even affectionate opinions of people by ethnic groups, I could probably come up with a couple of Lower Manhattan Italians I don't like, but my heart wouldn't be in it.

At Tiro, people seemed to stick to their own tables less than they might in an uptown club; Wally's friends often stopped to chat at our table, and sometimes sat down to join us for a double espresso. The food, of course, had nothing at all in common with the sort of club food that seems designed to reassure a guest that all members have descended from bona fide Puritans. A member of Tiro, setting aside his plate of roasted peppers to give the waiter room to put down the pasta e fagioli, might discuss standard American club food with a polite but slightly patronizing smile. Members of Tiro tended to take a strong, critical interest in what was served at the club. Wally told us that there had once been a ferocious controversy over a suggestion by one member that peanuts be included in the nut bowls at the bar—a suggestion that some other members believed would leave any respectable guest with the impression that Tiro a Segno had fallen into the hands of peasants or know-nothings.

"I happen to know that the Yale Club has peanuts at the bar," I said.

Wally shrugged and threw open his hands in a gesture that said, "Precisely my point. They don't know any better. Case closed."

MATT UMANOV

In the early 1970s, when my guitar store

was very small and located on a then-sleepy block of lower Bedford Street, we had well-known musician customers as well as the occasional clueless walk-in. On a particular day, a somewhat ragged-looking hippie-type kid walked in, took down a guitar from the display wall and started playing, quite badly. After ten minutes of torture, Susie, my wife at the time, and I were just on the verge of shutting this kid down and showing him the door when in walked Bob Dylan, a sometime regular there. Without saying a word, Bob picked up a guitar and started playing with the kid. They were, in a word, collectively awful, and if it hadn't been Bob, we would've tossed them both, on general principles. They never said a word to each other, just played together, and after about fifteen minutes the kid put down the guitar and left.

About a week later, the same kid walks back in, all excited, and says to Susie, "Do you know who I was just playing guitar with in Washington Square Park??!!?? David fucking PEEL!!!!" Now David Peel was the loudmouth screamer with the guitar who all over the city bellowed "HAVE A MARIJUANA!!" He was fairly well known in certain circles, as far away as Haight-Ashbury in San Francisco. So Susie looks at the kid and says, "Schmuck! Do you know who you were playing with in here last week? That was Bob Dylan!" And the kid says "Holy shit! And I thought those were *my* vibes!!" Never saw him again. Never asked Bob about it, either.

Outdoor Music, in Washington Square Park.
Photo by Weegee/Getty Images. 1956.

DAVID VAUGHAN

In the late '6os the Merce Cunningham

Studio was in an illegal sublet at 498 Third Avenue, a building that was going to be pulled down if it didn't fall down first. I read about Westbeth in the *New York Times* and called to ask if there was a space suitable for Merce to have a studio. There was, and Merce and I went over to look at it: the former auditorium in what had been the Bell Telephone Labs, where the first television transmission took place sometime in the early '3os. It was a space Merce might have dreamed of, with windows along both sides, looking out at the Hudson in one direction, and uptown toward the Empire State Building in the other. Then they told us what the rent would be, way beyond our means at that time. Thanks to Joan Davidson of the Kaplan Fund, one of the building's sponsors, an arrangement was made, and at the beginning of 1971, when Westbeth opened for business, the Cunningham Studio was installed there.

In those days I was the Studio secretary. Pat Richter, our wonderful class pianist, would run out to my office and say, "You have to come and look at the sunset over the Hudson River."

Merce, who loved to look out of windows and often saw movements of pedestrians that gave him ideas for choreography, had a view in his own office at the back of the Studio that included the Statue of Liberty.

We remained there for nearly forty years, until the Merce Cunningham Dance Company was disbanded and we vacated the Studio, offices, and storage spaces, to be taken over, in what seemed to many of us a supreme irony, by the Martha Graham company, which Merce had left in the mid-'4os to devote himself to his own work.

Merce created some seventy-five theater dances in that Studio, as well as ten video or film dances. Hundreds of dancers came through the daily technique classes and repertory workshops. For a period in the '7os when no theater in the city was available for company performances, Merce staged Events (collages of

Merce Cunningham in his Westbeth Studio. Photo by James Klosty. 1972.

excerpts from the repertory, including works in progress) in the Studio, which became a hot ticket.

When John Cage died in 1992, Merce returned to work the next day and resumed rehearsals on the piece he was making, *Enter*. Instead of a memorial for Cage, a huge party was given in the Studio, to which people came from far and wide in the United States, even from Europe. Merce sat in his usual corner, receiving visitors.

The day after Merce himself died, in July 2009, the Studio was open for classes as usual. People poured in all day long, and at the six o'clock class more than sixty people took the floor to perform the opening movement in a Cunningham technique class.

Merce loved that Studio: even on days when there were no classes or rehearsals, he would come in to work by himself. During the company's last farewell tour, the dancers would come back between trips for rehearsal and recuperation in the Studio, which was still full of his spirit.

ANNE WALDMAN

I grew up on MacDougal Street in Greenwich

Village, right below Houston. My mother lived in a house with other women whose men, husbands, lovers were off fighting the Nazis in Germany and other war zones. It was a bohemian household and continued that way even after our "nuclear family" evolved. I didn't meet my father until I was nearly nine months old. There is a photograph of us in Washington Square Park, my father in army dress with cap, and I am fiddling with one of his buttons. I often cite this as my first "luminous detail" for poetry. And a life in poetry.

My childhood in many ways was idyllic, creative, generative, so why was I obsessed with war? Many of my school friends had fathers who had also been off "fighting the Nazis" and my Jewish friends had family members killed by the Nazis, although we were not taught officially about the Holocaust at this tender age. My parents were agnostic/atheist and there was a terrific racial and religious tolerance in our house. When I came home insisting that I had "seen the devil" in the girls' bathroom, along with all my Catholic school friends, there was no rational talking down or denial of my experience.

My older brother Mark was a "folkie" who spent his Saturdays at Washington Square Park, which became an extension of our lives. Pete Seeger lived down the block and I attended his hootenannies in the park. And once Leadbelly—Huddie Ledbetter, the great iconic folk and blues singer who played a twelve-string guitar and sang a beautiful version of "Goodnight Irene"—came to our house and I sat on his lap.

I went to school around the corner on King Street, at Public School 8, later a school for "delinquent girls," and now a co-op apartment building. I remember the school guards at the corner helping children across the street, and later I was to wear the guard's plastic white band myself. I remember reading a poem on Arbor Day, which we celebrated with a little parade outside the school and then a tree planting. I remember a sense of civic pride. I remember writing a letter to Albert

Einstein and getting a response! But I also remember wearing a dog tag and having to take shelter under my desk with all the other children, of being warned about the Bomb and nuclear fallout. Of wondering, how could one survive a nuclear attack? How is that possible?

I refused to be a nihilist, however, and turned toward art, toward an alternative, toward a way to obviate fear. I credit the ambience of the Village in those days: the diversity of the neighborhood, and the way it accommodated an openly tolerant liberal stance. The atmosphere was more intimate, friendly, "consociational"—an anthropological term I admire, describing the coexisting of people, inter-generationally. We overlapped in so many ways, years ago, in the small grocery stores, in Arturo's Pizzeria, at the Greenwich House Children's Theater on Barrow Street where I took classes.

People were putting their lives together. Rents were cheap (we paid $40 a month on MacDougal Street). My father was going to school now on the GI Bill. Who ever wanted to go to war again? People had already been there and suffered. There wasn't so much posturing, and thrum and drumbeat.

I loved the snow days. No school. Being pulled on a sled to the park, wrapped up in a plaid woolen blanket.

Jive in the Park. Photo by Ernst Haas/Getty Images. 1955.

SEAN WILENTZ

The first Eighth Street Bookshop, at 32

West 8th, stood on the southeast corner of MacDougal. It had been a Womrath's, another long-gone New York institution, a chain of bookstores where you bought what they had in stock but where you also rented the very latest releases cheap, three days for a nickel (or maybe it was a quarter), a bargain if you could read fast enough. In 1947, my father Elias and his brother Ted bought out the 8th Street Womrath's and soon enough were stocking it with books of all publishers, as they later grandly put it in their ads. This meant that the shop carried really serious literary classics as well as the past, present, and (just maybe) future avant-garde. If you were looking for García Lorca or Lowell or *Paterson*, for the Fitts and Fitzgerald translations of Sophocles, for the existentialists or the playwrights of the absurd, for C. Wright Mills or Ayn Rand, you would go to their shop. And when the trade paperback revolution began soon thereafter—inspired by one of the shop's many friends, the young publisher Jason Epstein, who once told me that *he* was inspired by the bookshop—the brothers Wilentz took up the change right away.

By the time the Beat Generation had become the rage, the bookshop was well established—and the shop helped establish the Beats and their literary progeny. It wasn't just *Howl* and *On the Road*, but everything that the poet and kindred spirit Lawrence Ferlinghetti published at City Light Books in San Francisco; everything published by New Directions and Grove Press; everything, right down to the little magazines like *Neurotica*, *Yugen*, and *Big Table*. (Eli and Ted published books too, mainly poetry and history, under the imprint of Corinth Books.) A little later came the poetry from Black Mountain and the emerging New York School. The shop became a part-time employer, regular hangout, and convenient mail drop for poets and writers. I own, and have had framed, a sweet postcard that Jack Kerouac mailed from Brittany in the early 1960s, addressed to "Avrum" Ginsberg (and to my father, just in case), in care of the shop, comparing the Breton seascape photograph on the front to Big Sur. The card arrived postage due.

Eighth Street Bookshop at MacDougal Street. Photo by Robert Otter. 1965.

To understand the scene, you have to imagine 8th Street as it was then, the Main Street of the West Village, oxymoron though that might seem, filled with an amazing array of stores and eateries: classy men's clothiers; Sam Kramer's jewelers (upstairs); the honest-to-goodness 8th Street Deli; Nedick's; the Village Barn nightclub; a tiny gay boîte, Bon Soir, where Barbra Streisand would get her start; the venerable Jumble Shop restaurant; Discophile, the classical record store supreme. Busy during the day, 8th Street was so clogged at night it was actually difficult to move about. The bookshop (which stayed open until eleven) anchored the scene, as it continued to do after 1965, when the Wilentz brothers had the good sense to buy the building across the street at 17 West 8th, keeping them secure from rent-gouging and gaining a great deal more space—in time three whole floors of books.

I well remember the move to 17 West—Allen Ginsberg's lover, Peter Orlovsky, long-haired and wearing a mottled tam-o'-shanter, proved an amazingly strong lifter of cartons—and the party to celebrate the new store's opening, a bash filled with writers, artists, critics, and the local congressman, John V. Lindsay, with the Giuseppi Logan Trio providing the music. It was on a Sunday, February 21, the day after my fourteenth birthday, the day of my first glass of champagne. The festivities were jumping when the jolting news started filtering around that Malcolm X had been shot dead in Harlem. I remember seeing LeRoi Jones immediately depart, silent and shaken. (The next time I saw him in the shop, his name was Amiri Baraka.) That night, one phase of the '60s ended and another scarier and more frantic phase began, at one of the literary culture's epicenters, which by now I understood it was.

The 1960s into the 1970s was a very different time, the shop now a place with a reputation as (another ad proclaimed) a literary landmark. My father, who had taken sole ownership of the shop after he and his brother became estranged, came up with the idea of displaying books he and the staff thought notable, right up front, face (that is, front cover) out. There might be a volume of Richard Howard's poems next to the latest Philip Roth, which stood beneath a new Kafka translation, which was beside Erica Jong's *Fear of Flying*. Writers would stop in, faking nonchalance, to see if their new book had made the cut. It didn't necessarily help if you were a regular customer, but it didn't hurt, either.

My father, and the shop's exceptionally well-read managers and clerks, knew their own minds but also knew the tastes of their most loyal patrons. The more celebrated of those loyal patrons ran the gamut: in the earlier days, Delmore Schwartz might lumber in, or it might be Auden or Diane di Prima; later, Viva from Andy Warhol's Factory might be making a little scene at the front desk just as Dick Barnett of the Knicks was bumping his head trying to get through the front door. But this being the Village (let alone New York), nobody made a fuss; everybody was equal, or was supposed to be.

In 1976, an arsonist destroyed the place, leaving behind a nauseating mass of burned books, sodden from the fire hoses. My father, if only to save his sanity, rebuilt; there was a benefit at which Allen Ginsberg composed, on the spot and on the tongue, a wonderful poem, "The Burning of the Eighth Street Bookshop," which nobody taped; and there was a sense of indomitability. But the street was changing amid the city's crack-fueled dolor, and my father could see the writing on the wall. When he closed the shop in 1979 he placed in the window a thank-you note to the writers, readers, and artists of Greenwich Village, bidding them a long and productive future.

Thirty-five years later, perfect strangers, hearing my last name, bemoan the bookshop's demise, as if my family could have withstood the gigantic commercial and technological forces that were already looming in 1979. What they are really saying is that there will never be anyplace quite like the Eighth Street Bookshop ever again, and they are right.

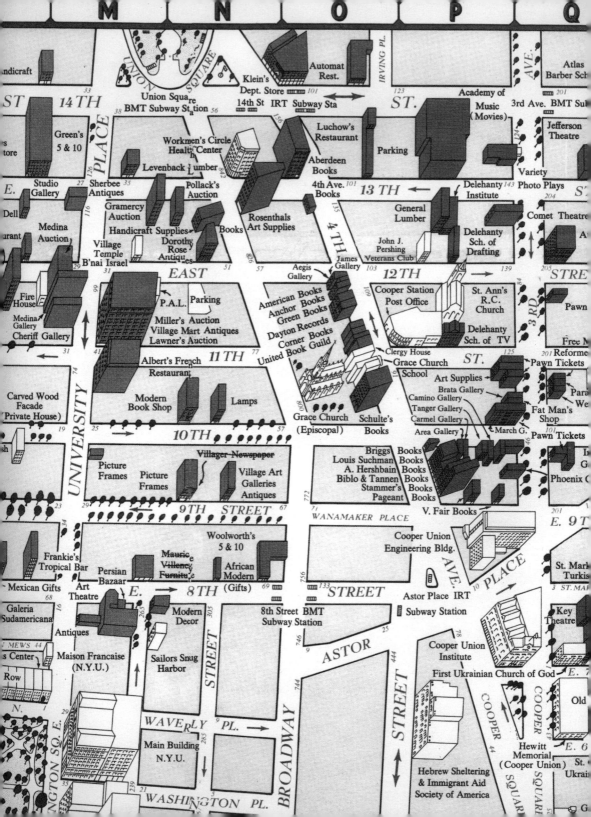

ABOUT THE CONTRIBUTORS

JONATHAN ADLER started his namesake ceramics line in 1994 and is also known for home furnishings and design. His latest book is *100 Ways to Happy Chic Your Life.*

Performance artist **PENNY ARCADE** is also a playwright, director, actor, and a founder of the Lower East Side Biography Project.

MARIO BATALI is an award-winning chef, restaurateur, author, and television host.

LAUREN BELFER has written two acclaimed novels: *City of Light* and *A Fierce Radiance.*

ANDREW BERMAN has served as the executive director of the Greenwich Village Society for Historic Preservation since 2002. He was named one of the "100 Most Influential" by *New York* magazine and nominated by *Vanity Fair* to its "Hall of Fame" for his preservation work with GVSHP.

AVIS BERMAN is an art historian whose many books include *Rebels on Eighth Street: Juliana Force and the Whitney Museum of American Art.*

JENNIFER FINNEY BOYLAN, a leading transgender advocate, teaches English at Colby College. Her most recent book is *Stuck in the Middle with You: A Memoir of Parenting in Three Genders.*

Artist **TOM BURCKHARDT** curated the "404 East 14" exhibition at the Tibor de Nagy in 2013. He has shown his work at that gallery as well as at Caren Golden Fine Art and the Pierogi Gallery.

GRAYDON CARTER, editor of *Vanity Fair*, is also an author, producer, and restaurateur.

MARTHA CLARKE is a director and choreographer of theater, dance, and opera whose numerous honors include a MacArthur Award.

Film, television, and stage actor **PATRICIA CLARKSON** has received two Emmys for her work in *Six Feet Under* and an Academy Award nomination for *Pieces of April.*

Since 1972 **KAREN COOPER** has been director of Film Forum, a renowned cinema for independent film and repertory programming.

Columnist, author, and fashion authority **SIMON DOONAN** is creative ambassador for Barneys New York. His latest book is *The Asylum: A Collage of Couture Reminiscences.*

LINDA ELLERBEE is an award-winning television producer, journalist, and author.

LARRY FAGIN is a poet, editor, publisher, and teacher of poetry and writing. *Complete Fragments*, his fifteenth collection of poems, was published in 2012.

KAREN FINLEY is a performance artist, author, poet, illustrator, actor, singer, and teacher. Her most recent work is *Catch 23: Broken Negative.*

Emmy Award-winner **TOM FONTANA** is a writer and producer whose credits include *St. Elsewhere, Homicide, Life on the Streets, Oz,* and Netflix's *Borgia.*

Historian, writer, and broadcaster **AMANDA FOREMAN** is the author of the best-selling books *Georgiana, Duchess of Devonshire* and *A World on Fire: Britain's Crucial Role in the American Civil War.*

A celebrated artist, **JANE FREILICHER** has painted images of the Village for more than fifty years. Her most recent show, *Jane Freilicher: Painter Among Poets,* was held in 2013 at the Tibor de Nagy Gallery.

Author and essayist **BETTY FUSSELL** writes about film, theater, and food. Her eleventh book is *Raising Steaks: The Life and Times of American Beef.*

MARGARET HALSEY GARDINER is executive director of the 1832 Merchant's House Museum, a National Historic Landmark on East 4th Street.

MALCOLM GLADWELL, a staff writer at *The New Yorker,* is the author of many acclaimed books, including *The Tipping Point.* His most recent work is *David and Goliath.*

MIMI GROSS is a painter, sculptor, installation artist, teacher, and costume and set designer. She has shown her work in dozens of exhibitions since the late 1950s.

The many award-winning works of playwright **JOHN GUARE** include *The House of Blue Leaves, Six Degrees of Separation,* and the recent production of *3 Kinds of Exile.*

ROBERT HAMMOND is the co-founder, with Joshua David, of Friends of the High Line. For their work in saving the railway, they were awarded the Jane Jacobs medal in 2010. Robert was also awarded the Rome Prize by the American Academy in Rome in 2009.

NAT HENTOFF is a columnist, historian, novelist, and music critic, who received a National Press Foundation Award for Distinguished Contributions to Journalism.

DAVE HILL is a writer, musician, actor, and comedian who contributes to NPR's *This American Life*. St. Martin's Press recently published his book *Tasteful Nudes: . . . And Other Misguided Attempts at Personal Growth and Validation*.

TONY HISS is a writer, lecturer, planning and environmental consultant, and the author of *The Experience of Place*. His most recent book is *In Motion: The Experience of Travel*.

BOB HOLMAN is a poet, professor, and founder of the Bowery Poetry Club.

JAC HOLZMAN is the founder of Elektra Records, introducing Judy Collins, Phil Ochs, The Doors, Paul Butterfield Blues Band, Love, Queen, Carly Simon, Bread, Harry Chapin, and numerous others. He was inducted into the Rock and Roll Hall of Fame in 2011.

Poet **HETTIE JONES** is the author of numerous works, including poetry collections, books for children, and a memoir, *How I Became Hettie Jones*. She teaches at The New School.

DONNA KARAN, recipient of the Lifetime Achievement Award of the Council of Fashion Designers of America, is founder of the Urban Zen Foundation.

JONATHAN NED KATZ, an artist and author of books on sexual history, recently published *Coming of Age in Greenwich Village: A Memoir with Paintings*.

ROB KAUFELT is the owner of Murray's Cheese, the oldest cheese shop in Manhattan.

LENNY KAYE, a musician, songwriter, music producer, critic, and author, has performed and recorded with Patti Smith since 1974. They played the final concert at CBGB the night it closed in 2006.

BRAD KESSLER is an award-winning novelist and author of the memoir *Goat Song: A Seasonal Life, A Short History of Herding and the Art of Making Cheese*.

The late **ED KOCH** was a lifelong New Yorker best known for his three terms as the mayor of New York City, from 1978 to 1989.

RALPII LEE organized the first Greenwich Village Halloween Parade in 1974. He is the designer of masks and large puppets for major theater and dance companies across the country and is the longtime artist-in-residence at the Cathedral of St. John the Divine.

JOHN LEGUIZAMO, an award-winning actor, producer, voice artist, playwright, author, and comedian, is the subject of a PBS documentary, *Tales from a Ghetto Klown*.

ANITA LO is the owner and chef of the Michelin-starred restaurant Annisa and the author of *Cooking Without Borders*.

PETER LONGO owns and runs Porto Rico Importing Co., a family coffee business founded in 1907.

JESSE MALIN is a musician, writer, and DJ who has fronted New York City bands Heart Attack and D Generation. He now records as a solo artist.

Musician, composer, author, and educator **WYNTON MARSALIS** is artistic director of Jazz at Lincoln Center. His honors include nine Grammy Awards, the National Medal of Arts, and the Pulitzer Prize for Music.

GEORGE MATTESON has worked and written on and about the water all his life. He is the author of *Tugboats of New York: An Illustrated History*.

Photographer **DONA ANN McADAMS** has shown at the Museum of Modern Art and the Whitney Museum of American Art. Her performance work, *Caught in the Act*, was published as a monograph by *Aperture*.

CAROLYN CAPSTICK MEEHAN owned the well-loved children's shop Peanut Butter & Jane for twenty-seven years and is at work on a historical novel set in Greenwich Village.

THOMAS MEEHAN has written the books for nearly a dozen Broadway musicals and won Tony awards for *Annie*, *The Producers*, and *Hairspray*.

Acclaimed fashion designer **ISAAC MIZRAHI** is also an actor, television personality, theatrical costume designer, and the subject of the award-winning documentary *Unzipped*.

PETER MYERS is the founder of the British grocery store Myers of Keswick, a family business.

RON PADGETT is a teacher, translator, editor, and author of more than twenty collections of poetry.

IOANNIS PAPPOS is a writer, management consultant, and fisherman.

Architect **JAMES STEWART POLSHEK** founded Polshek Partnership. He and his wife, **ELLYN POLSHEK**, have lived in the Village for fifty-three years.

LOU REED is a rock musician, writer, and photographer. The former frontman for the Velvet Underground has published four books of photography.

MARK RUSSELL was the artistic director of PS 122 for more than twenty years. Now with the Public Theater, he is the creator of the annual Under the Radar Festival.

Artist **JOOP SANDERS**, an Abstract Expressionist, exhibited his paintings in the legendary Ninth Street Show in 1951 and continues to paint today.

MARTICA SAWIN is an art historian, critic, curator of exhibitions, and author of many books and essays on twentieth-century artists.

MIMI SHERATON was the restaurant critic for *The New York Times* from 1975 to 1983 and writes often about food and life. Her latest works are *The German Cookbook* and *Eating My Words: An Appetite for Life.*

Actor and model **BROOKE SHIELDS** has appeared in film, theater, and television. An author of several works, including *The New York Times* bestseller *Down Came the Rain,* she is currently writing her third children's book.

WILLIAM SOFIELD is the principal of Studio Sofield Inc., a multi-disciplinary design studio. In 2010 he received the National Design Award for Interior Design.

RAYMOND SOKOLOV is a former editor at *The New York Times* and the *Wall Street Journal.* His latest book is *Steal the Menu: A Memoir of Forty Years in Food.*

Author and lecturer **ANDREW SOLOMON** is the recipient of a National Book Award. His most recent work is the best-selling *Far from the Tree: Parents, Children, and the Search for Identity.*

JUDITH STONEHILL has written a series of books on the city published by Rizzoli, including *New York's Unique & Unexpected Places.*

PAUL TAYLOR is the founding principal and president of Stonehill & Taylor Architects.

CALVIN TRILLIN has written for *The New Yorker* since 1963 and has been *The Nation's* "Deadline Poet" since 1990. His latest book is *Dog Fight: The 2012 Presidential Campaign in Verse.*

MATT UMANOV is the founder of Matt Umanov Guitars, a shop that has been selling and repairing stringed instruments, new and old, since 1965.

DAVID VAUGHAN is the dance archivist for the Merce Cunningham Dance Company. He has written several books and recently produced the iPad app *Merce Cunningham: 65 Years.*

ANNE WALDMAN has published more than forty collections of poetry, including *The Iovis Trilogy,* which won the PEN USA Award in 2012. She is a founder of The Poetry Project, received a Guggenheim Fellowship in 2013, and is a Chancellor of the Academy of American Poets.

SEAN WILENTZ is a professor of American History at Princeton University. His books include *The Rise of American Democracy: From Jefferson to Lincoln* and *Bob Dylan in America.*

ILLUSTRATION CREDITS

BERENICE ABBOTT. Page 120: *Jefferson Market Court and 447-461 Sixth Avenue*, 1938. Courtesy of the Museum of the City of New York.

MILTON AVERY. Page 180: *Portrait of Chaim Gross*, 1944. Oil on canvas. Photo of painting taken by Jacob Burckhardt. Courtesy of the Milton Avery Estate, the Renee and Chaim Gross Foundation, New York, and the Artists Rights Society (ARS), New York.

FREDERICK BROSEN. Page 8: *West 10th Street* (detail), 2012. Page 81: *East Sixth Street Synagogue*, 2010. Page 172-173: *Gansevoort Street* (detail), 2007. All are watercolors on paper. Courtesy of Hirschl and Adler Gallery, New York.

RUDY BURCKHARDT. Page 27: *Astor Place*, 1948. Gelatin silver print. Page 69: *Jane Street Area* (detail), 1958. Oil on canvas. Private collection. Courtesy of Tibor de Nagy Gallery, New York.

WILLIAM S. BURROUGHS. Page 44: *Portait of Allen Ginsberg*, 1953. Courtesy of the Allen Ginsberg Estate, New York.

MORRIS ENGEL. Page 155: *Boy Reading Ha Ha Comic Book*, 1947. Copyright Morris Engel 1999. Courtesy of the Orkin/Engel Film and Photo Archive.

LAWRENCE FAHEY. Endpapers and Page 174: *Greenwich Village Map* (detail), 1961. Private collection.

TONY FITZPATRICK. Page 33: *Washington Square Serenade*, 2008. Drawing/Collage. Courtesy Pierogi Gallery, Brooklyn. Art used for album of Steve Earle's *Washington Square Serenade*.

JANE FREILICHER. Page 54: *City at Twilight*, 2010. Collection of Deborah S. Pease. Page 139: *The City in Pink and Gray*, 2006. Both are oil on linen paintings. Courtesy of Tibor de Nagy Gallery, New York.

DAVID GAHR. Page 78: *Izzy Young in NYC*, 1960. Courtesy of Getty Images.

DANIEL GERDES. Page 24: *Pencil/Charcoal*, 2008. Page 136: *Paint Brushes*, 2008. Courtesy of the New York Studio School.

ALLEN GINSBERG. Page 132: *Mary Help of Christians R. C. Church*, 1985. Page 135: *Backyard Gardens*, 1984. Courtesy of the Allen Ginsberg Estate, New York.

Portrait of Chaim Gross. Painting by Milton Avery. 1944.

GVSHP ARCHIVES. Pages 184: *Brevoort Hotel* photograph, 1954. New York Bound Collection.

ERNST HAAS. Page 166: *Jive in the Park*, 1955. Courtesy of Getty Images.

ANDREW JONES. Page 30: *Charles Street Portals*, 2005. Page 53: *West 11th Street Railing*, 2005. Page 119: *Hudson Street Cornices*, 2003. Page 144: *West 11th Street Stoops*, 1999. Oil on canvas paintings. Courtesy of the George Billis Gallery, New York.

JAMES KLOSTY. Page 163: *Merce Cunningham in his Westbeth Studio*, 1972. Courtesy of the artist.

LEGUIZAMO FAMILY COLLECTION. Page 99: *Mambo Mouth* poster, 1991.

SAUL LEITER. Page 50: *Snow*, 1960. Page 29: *Postmen*, 1952. Chromogenic dye coupler prints. Copyright Saul Leiter. Courtesy of the Howard Greenberg Gallery, New York.

LONGO FAMILY COLLECTION. Page 103: *Rose Longo and her daughter Mary Elizabeth*, 1944.

MICHAEL MAGILL. Page 85: *Washington Square*, 1993. Courtesy of the artist.

JACK MANNING. Page 87: *Drugstore Crows*, 1966. Courtesy of Getty Images.

DONA ANN McADAMS. Page 49: *Alphabet City*, 1987. Page 112: *Alphabet City*, 1986. Courtesy of the artist.

FRED W. McDARRAH. Page 93: *Ed Koch in Democratic Party Office*, 1963. Courtesy of Getty Images.

RUTH ORKIN. Page 115: *The Cardplayers*, 1947. Copyright Ruth Orkin 1981. Courtesy of the Orkin/Engel Film and Photo Archive.

ROBERT OTTER. Book cover: *Café Figaro* (detail), 1965. Page 14: *Café Wha?*, 1963. Page 19: *Ruggiero's Fish Market* (detail), 1965. Page 65: *Bleecker Street Cinema*, 1965. Page 70: *Washington Square Arch*, 1962. Page 156: *Café Figaro* (detail), 1965. Page 169: *8th Street Bookshop at MacDougal Street*, 1965. Copyright Ned Otter, 2005. All photos courtesy of Ned Otter.

LARRY RIVERS, in collaboration with **FRANK O'HARA**. Page 17: *Portrait and Poem Painting*, 1961. Oil on canvas. Private collection. Courtesy of Tibor de Nagy Gallery.

PETER RUTA. Page 82: *Pier 49 at Bank Street*, 1991. Oil on canvas. Page 130: *Blimp above New York*, 1989. Oil on canvas. Courtesy of the artist. Page 188–189: *Downtown* (detail), 1961. Gouache on paper.

TONY SARG. Page 143: *A Map of Greenwich Village* (detail), 1934. Courtesy of GVSHP Archives. New York Bound Collection.

SHELLEY SECCOMBE. Page 127: *Swimmer, Back Flip*, 1979. Page 147: *Rotterdam Passing Pier 51*, 1978. Courtesy of the artist.

SAUL STEINBERG. Page 94: *Bleecker Street*, 1971. Ink, pencil, colored pencil, and crayon on paper, 29 ⅜ x 22 ⅜ inches. Private collection. Courtesy of The Saul Steinberg Foundation/Artists Rights Society (ARS), New York.

ALEXANDRA STONEHILL. Pages 4, 6, 13, 33, 37, 38, 43, 59, 75, 150: Greenwich Village photographs, 2013. Courtesy of the artist.

ADELE URSONE. Page 109: *From the Barge*, 2008. Oil on board. Courtesy of the artist.

ALFREDO VALENTE. Page 60: *Chaim Gross in his Studio*, 1938. Courtesy of the Renee and Chaim Gross Foundation, New York.

JACK VARTOOGIAN. Page 106: *Wynton Marsalis at the Village Vanguard* (detail), 1993. Courtesy of Getty Images.

WEEGEE (Arthur Felig). Page 160: *Outdoor Music*, 1942. International Center of Photography Collection. Courtesy of Getty Images.

Artwork without attribution (artists or photographers not known): Page 20: Vintage Botanical Engraving. Page 66: High Line Photograph, 1936. Page 88: John Coltrane Jazz Album, 1960. Page 140: Photo of the Fourth Avenue Bookstores, c. 1940s. All of the above are in private collections.

SOME BOOKS ABOUT THE VILLAGE

For those who want to read more Village stories:

Kafka Was the Rage: A Greenwich Village Memoir by Anatole Broyard. 1993. The author took Meyer Schapiro's art history classes at The New School and hung out with other young writers in the bar at the San Remo. He opened a secondhand bookshop on Cornelia Street, in 1946, a time when "there were people in the Village who had more books than money."

The Diaries of Dawn Powell 1931–1965. Edited by Tim Page. 1998. Engaging journals of a writer known for her satirical novels. "The Village is my creative oxygen," Powell noted in her diary pages, writing that she had "started a novel about Café Lafayette. Wrote seven pages." This book was titled *The Wicked Pavilion*, published in 1954. The actual Lafayette, a favorite of the literary crowd, had been demolished the year before.

Just Kids by Patti Smith. 2010. A lyrical account of traversing the city when very young, in the late 1960s and 70s, before becoming a musician and poet. There was a "thick psychedelic atmosphere" on St. Marks Place, breakfast for two cost fifty cents at the Waverly Diner, and "one could still feel the characters of Henry James and the presence of the author himself" in Washington Square.

Joe Gould's Secret by Joseph Mitchell. 1964. A fascinating profile of a quintessential Village eccentric. Gould, a Harvard graduate from a distinguished family, led the life of a derelict, sleeping in doorways and panhandling in Village hangouts while supposedly writing his nine-million-word magnum opus, "An Oral History of Our Time." He was known as the resident bohemian of Minetta Tavern.

Washington Square by Henry James. 1881. A heartbreaking story with complex moral questions. Much of the drama— in which a guileless young woman is dominated by her tyrannical father— takes place in a handsome red brick house, "solid and honorable," on the north side of the Square. Henry James was born just steps away from here, on Washington Place, and his grandmother lived in one of the red brick houses on the Square.

Brevoort Hotel, on Fifth Avenue and East 8th Street. 1954. The Brevoort was demolished the same year this photograph was taken.

Limelight: A Greenwich Village Photography Gallery and Coffeehouse in the Fifties by Helen Gee. 1997. The author created this legendary place near Sheridan Square, at 91 Seventh Avenue South. Robert Franks sold his photographs here for twenty-five dollars, Eugene Smith and Edward Weston for fifty. "At one table you'd find Philippe Halsman drinking coffee with friends; at another Arnold Newman; . . . and Weegee, at no table, just roaming around."

John Sloan's New York Scene: 1906–1913. At the time this diary begins, Sloan was 34 years old and had never sold a painting. He later became famous as "the leading paint-and-canvas historian of New York," and painted the Village over and over again: the Sixth Avenue Elevated, McSorley's Bar, a movie theater on Carmine Street, and children playing in Washington Square Park. His first one-man exhibition was in 1916 at the Whitney Studio on 8th Street.

Those Days by Hamilton Fish Armstrong. 1963. Recollections of growing up on West 10th Street during the 1890s, only a block away from a firehouse with a horse-drawn engine. Nearby, next to Grace Church on Broadway, was Fleischmann's bakery, "a place to stop at the right seasons for hot cross buns, election cake, Christmas cinnamon stars, and New Year's cookies with caraway seeds."

Elizabeth Street by Laurie Fabiano. 2010. A vivid novel based on the author's own family—in particular her indomitable great-grandmother, an Italian immigrant from Calabria who arrived on Elizabeth Street in January 1903. It was a neighborhood of Southern Italians, with opera buffa performed at the Teatro Villa Giulia on Grand Street. It was also a time when the notorious Black Hand, gangs of vicious criminals, terrorized the new immigrants.

Greenwich Village: Today & Yesterday. Photographs by Berenice Abbott. Text by Henry W. Lanier. 1949. The sixty-four pages of photographs are the reason to search for this rare book, as they tell a story of the Village in the 1940s. The images show the sculptor Isamu Noguchi in his studio on MacDougal Alley,

ACKNOWLEDGMENTS

The Greenwich Village Society for Historic Preservation expresses boundless gratitude to everyone who participated in *Greenwich Village Stories*. We extend special thanks to the writers of these engaging stories and to all the artists who contributed their captivating work.

In particular, thanks to Judith Stonehill, who initiated the project and was the driving force in creating this book. Very special thanks to Cynthia Penney for her skills as an editor *par excellence*, and to the other diligent members of GVSHP's Editorial Committee: Justine Leguizamo, Fred Wistow, Tom Birchard, Eric Brown, Toby Cox, Matt Umanov, and Andrew Berman. Many thanks to Alexandra Stonehill for researching and selecting the artwork in the book. Extra thanks to Drew Durniak for providing immeasurable help in keeping track of the book's sixty-six stories and a thousand details.

Many thanks for the very generous support of Eric Brown at the Tibor de Nagy Gallery, Sean A. Cavanaugh at the Milton Avery Estate, as well as Mary Engel at the Orkin/Engel Photo Archives, Margit Erb at the Howard Greenberg Gallery, Constance Evans at the New York Studio School, Susan Greenberg Fisher at the Renee and Chaim Gross Foundation, Peter Hale at the Allen Ginsberg Trust, Nilda Rivera at MCNY, Sheila Schwartz at the Saul Steinberg Foundation, Dunham Townsend and Shelley Farmer at the Hirschl & Adler Gallery, and Adam Welch at Greenwich House Pottery.

Thanks to so many Villagers and others who were helpful: Mary Ann Arisman, Adam Baumgold, Aimee Bell, David Bressman, Barbara Cohen, Steve Earle, Elizabeth Ely, Wendy Gleason, Cassie Glover, Karin and Timothy Greenfield-Sanders, Arthur Levin, Michael Magill, Vals Osborne, Jeffrey Podolsky, Suzanne Ruta, Allan Sperling, Mia Ting, Bernice Tsai, and Sheryl Woodruff.

To everyone on the Rizzoli team, thanks and appreciation—especially to Ellen R. Cohen, an extraordinary editor, and Willy Wong, the brilliant book designer of *Greenwich Village Stories*.

All the royalties for *Greenwich Village Stories* will be given to the Greenwich Village Society for Historic Preservation.

Following page: *Downtown* (detail). Painting by Peter Ruta. 1961.

First published in the
United States of America
in 2014 by Universe Publishing
A Division of Rizzoli
International Publications, Inc.
300 Park Avenue South
New York, NY 10010
www.rizzoliusa.com

Design: Willy Wong
Rizzoli Editor: Ellen Cohen

Library of Congress Control
Number: 2013950557

ISBN 978-0-7893-2722-2

Printed in China

2014 2015 2016 2017 / 10 9 8 7 6 5 4 3 2 1

Grateful acknowledgment is made
to the following for permission to
include copyrighted material in
Greenwich Village Stories:

Ron Padgett's poem was published
in *My Collected Poems* in 2013 by
Coffee House Press.

Calvin Trillin's story was published
in his book *Family Man* in 1998 by
Farrar Straus and Giroux.

Greenwich Village Stories is part of a
series of New York Bound books.

Contact GVSHP at:
Greenwich Village Society
for Historic Preservation
232 East 11th Street
New York, NY 10003
www.gvshp.org

WEST

14th St. IND Subway Sta.
8th Ave. BMT Subway Sta.

Piedmont
Rest.

Josef
Handb

St. Bernard's
R.C. Church

Pappas
Restaurant

Parking

La Casita
(Gifts)
Spanish
Books

Me
Ch

SAYVILLE LIBRARY
88 GREENE AVENUE
SAYVILLE, NY 11

St. Bernard's
School

JACKSON
SQUARE

Public
Library

339

301

Chateau
Cervantes

253

W.

Dorg
Re

W.   13 TH   ST.

APR 0 9 2014

Shell
Gas Station

ST.

AVE.

Jack Barry's
Bar

GANSEVOORT ST.

650

342

Mobile
Gas Station

Sea Colony
Restaurant

ST.

235

HORATIO

35

636

Cathy's
Gifts

31

Greenwich Village
Humane League

40

Frisco's
Bar

331

STREET

823

Arent's
Antiques

57

Beatrice Inn
Rest.

381

Village
Book Store

Waverly I
Restaura

JANE

807

622

Hour Glass
Antiques

293

12 TH

319

WEST

STREET

S
in th
(E

House where
Alexander Hamilton
died after a duel
with Aaron Burr.

309

Bank St.
College of
Education

41

51

299

58

317

8 TH

Jai-Alai Restaurant

255

281

621

Village
Nursing Home

ABINGDON
SQUARE

253

Lobster Roll Restaurant

Greenwich Village
Fish Market

4 TH

55

BETHUNE

6   ST.

16

777

584

BLEEKER

283

Elan
Gallery

309

Congreg
Darech A

BANK

101

769

97

11TH

299

Dorgene
Bar

81

383

White Horse Tavern

311

HUDSO

Salvation Army
Store

VAN

Fred Va

Savat Nova

169

749